CRAFTY CHICA'S GUIDE TO ARTFUL SEWING

CRAFTY CHICA'S GUIDE TO ARTFUL SEWING

Fabu-Low-Sew Projects for the Everyday Crafter

KATHY CANO-MURILLO

POTTER
CRAFT

NEW YORK

Published in the United States
by Potter Craft, an imprint of
the Crown Publishing Group,
a division of Random House, Inc.,
New York.
www.crownpublishing.com
wwww.pottercraft.com

POTTER CRAFT and colophon
is a registered trademark of
Random House, Inc.

Library of Congress
Cataloging-in-Publication Data

Cano-Murillo, Kathy.
Crafty Chica's guide to artful
sewing : fabu-low-sew projects
for the everyday crafter /
Kathy Cano-Murillo. — Ist ed.
p.   cm.
ISBN 978–0–307-40666–8
I. Fancy work. 2. Textile crafts.
I. Title.
TT750.C256   2009
746 — dc22
2008030252

ISBN: 978-0-307-40666-8
Printed in China

Design by Laura Palese

I0 9 8 7 6 5 4 3 2 I

First Edition

This book is dedicated to my Nana Cano and my Nana Jauregui—two creative, funny, insightful, devoted women. I hope to carry on their sparkly spirit in this life and the next!

CONTENTS

INTRODUCTION

I'm not a SEAMSTRESS.

But I am a thread artist. A freak for fibers. A hardcore material mama. I'm *loca* for lace, buttons, and any trim that sparkles more than a Christmas ornament. Don't believe me? Here's some irrefutable evidence:

I once cut up all of my husband's favorite Latin-themed T-shirts to create one heck of a fabuloso quilt. In one night.

. . . .

I've bought thirsty beach towels only to whack them apart to make funky summer totes.

. . . .

I've snipped wild-looking buttons off a brand-new coat just to use them on a fabric collage purse. The coat is still in my closet, with no buttons. But I do have an awesomely accessorized purse!

. . . .

I once stitched 283 buttons on the front of my jeans jacket. I know it looked cool because someone stole it off my barstool at a nightclub.

. . . .

As a kid, I cut up my Nina Josie's faux fur trim on her evening coat—just to hand-sew a dozen furry mini-plush creatures. Woo-ee! Did I get in so much trouble from my parents for that one!

See? I love to sew. But again, I'm not a seamstress.

Sometimes I don't use a measuring tape, but I always have plenty of them on hand anyway in case I want use them as trim on a lampshade. I've never used a pattern (except for seventh-grade home ec class), but I have used the schematic tissue sheets to découpage the outside of my sewing basket. I've never taken a formal class, but I have a powerful thread-friendly prayer that I recite every time that needle punctures through whatever surface I happen to be "drawing" on.

A seam ripper? Of course! But if I've lost it, a safety pin will do just fine. No, I don't own a serger, but I'd like to someday. And, yes. I fear *the Bobbin*. I don't, however, let it stop me from working my zigzag function like Gisele Bündchen on the runway.

As with anything else in my life, I refuse to let my doubts get the best of me. But I wasn't always so confident on the subject of stitches. Even though my Nana Cano was a talented professional seamstress, and I knew I had her spirit in me, I shied away from sewing because I never thought I could do it justice. I'd watch craft shows where amazing artists would parade out their gorgeous multifaceted quilts. I'd watch fashion runway shows on the news, admiring the crisp seams and detail. I wanted to join in the fun, but I let these things intimidate me.

My husband caught on to my secret fantasy of becoming a master sewer, and after my Nana Cano passed away, he surprised me with a generic $100 machine. I took it out of the box and admired it, yet wondered how in the world I would be able to use it. I remember reading the bobbin-threading directions over and over again. For my first project, I decided on a place mat purse. One fabric place mat, fold in half, stitch up the sides. Easy. I added a strap—and there was my first masterpiece!

I've since challenged myself to make tougher pieces, still totally freeform. I call it kamikaze style—just dive in, nose first, and give it 100 percent of your passion. Conquering the machine is so exhilarating and freeing that I want to share the experience. As an artist, I feel empowered, rebellious even, every time I step on that pedal.

You can do it, too! This book is all about shortcuts and head starts. Simple stitches used in clever applications. I want you to feel confident and talented enough to branch off on your own textile journey.

I'm not only going to hold your hand, I'll sprinkle good-luck glitter above your head. We'll dabble in image transfers, fabric collage, easy-breezy trims, and so much more. And it will all turn out vibrant, beautiful, and totally and completely *you* because there are no strict rules to follow. All the ideas in this book can be altered any way you like. Think of them as a simple guide to inspire you.

This book isn't about building an entire wardrobe; it's about using sewing as a way to enrich your creative process, add texture to your art and your life, and just have fun. Yes, all the basics are here for your reference, but the idea is to let yourself roam beyond the rules and be proud of what you invent and discover.

Sewing is like anything else that starts out rough—riding a bike, roller skating, skateboarding, singing in public, writing an essay. At first, it's tricky. Your palms will sweat, but once you get the hang of it, and discover all the glorious embellishment opportunities, you will appreciate—and celebrate—what artful sewing is all about!

And you don't need to be a seamstress to know that.

REASONS TO SEW

Throughout my crafty adventures, I've met so many people who tell me they want to learn to sew "someday"—but then spew out a laundry list of reasons why they can't—or rather, won't. Well, people—this chica is all about positive thinking. Enough of the excuses. There is a reason you are reading this very sentence at this moment. It's destiny—you were meant to sew! Before you shrug off that thought, read my reasons below why we all need to celebrate this art form. Make a photocopy of this list and hang it up in your room or office to remind you. Decorate it with glitter so it catches your attention until you finally break out the needle and thread.

- IT'S A SKILL YOU CAN BRAG ABOUT. Life is short, and there are so many activities to indulge in. Bungee jumping is overrated—learn to sew instead! You'll be able to mend and alter clothing on a whim. And just think: Once you master your first project, you can officially shout to the world, "I sew!"

- YOU WILL LEARN SOMETHING NEW ABOUT YOURSELF. Working with a needle and thread will make you discover a whole new dimension to your personality. The way you tackle critical thinking, choose color combinations, the direction in which you insert straight pins, even the way you snip—it will all come to be your signature style.

- MEET NEW FRIENDS. Once you take your first stitch, you will have bonded with a gazillion other threadheads, many of them in your own 'hood. You can connect with them for inspiration, tips, or just to have company while you create.

- NEW PLACES TO SHOP. Hello, fabric store! You thought trying on shoes gave you goosebumps—try draping delicious fabric over your body and imagining what to make! The options are limitless. Whether you plan to use it to make a couture dress or a simple table covering, the thrill is the same.

- HONORING YOUR ELDERS. Many of us have moms (yes, dads, too), aunts, and grandmas who work a machine like nobody's business. Well, we have their genes, energy, and spirit within us. Think of how proud they would be to see you whipping out that measuring tape!

- TEACHING OTHERS. It doesn't matter how much experience you have, once you take up sewing, I'd bet my favorite pair of pinking shears that you will give advice to others. So embrace what you learn and appreciate it. Knowledge is power!

- DESIGN CUSTOM WORK YOU LOVE. You'll be able to take bits and pieces from concepts you love and incorporate them into one ultra-

Stitch in Time

I was trying to sew some shorts for my seven-year-old son. I laid out the pattern on some Popeye comic strip material. I realized that the way the pattern directed me to lay it out wasted a lot of material. So I moved the pattern pieces around and found that I saved almost ¼ yard (23cm) of material. Cool! I cut and sewed the pieces together. I held up the finished product and realized that the comic strip was upside down on the front of the shorts. I told my son I did it on purpose so he could read the comics when he was sitting down. "Cool!" he said, and wore them proudly! Problem solved.

—LINDA SELNICK,
Fresno, California

fantastic piece of art or clothing. It will be tailor-made to your exact style at a price you can afford.

- GIFTING. This is my favorite aspect of creating art—the ability to give and share. You can take any kind of fabric and create something meaningful and useful.

- SHATTER SELF-DOUBTS. If you can tackle sewing, you'll learn that it wasn't so hard after all. Think about all the other things in life that you've missed out on and give them a second thought. Hey, maybe bungee jumping would be fun!

THE NEVER-ENDING WORLD OF FABRIC

Some chicas swoon over expensive purses, designer shoes, or shiny jewelry.

I'm all about the fabric. But it's easy to become overwhelmed by all the choices. My advice is to shop for one project at a time. Think of *Project Runway*. Each designer sketches an idea, and then selects the perfect foundation. That process will help you stay focused. Here are some starting points to consider.

TYPES OF FABRICS

Canvas, toile, muslin, quilted, cashmere, denim, silk, suede . . . Geez—so much to choose from! OK, here is my secret. I love to sew easy projects that look like I spent hours on them. One of my tricks is to use fabric that already has stitching, sequins, or other embellishments on it. It adds texture to your design without any extra sweat. I find cotton fabrics rock because they are a surefire success. If you make a mistake, it's easy

> ### *Stitch in* Time
>
> When I was in high school I took home economics. I chose to sew a purple sweatshirt dress (it was the '80s), with snaps up the front. The fabric was thick and bulky, and the sewing machine refused to cooperate. When I tried to "set" the sleeves, they turned out lumpy in the armpit every time. Finally, when everyone had left the class, my teacher ripped out the seam for the third time, sewed it herself (perfectly) and made me swear that I wouldn't tell anyone!
>
> —RHONDA SHYMKO,
> Saskatoon, Saskatchewan (Canada)

to take the seams out and re-sew without anyone ever knowing. There are many types of cottons, such as chintz, eyelet, muslin, and shirting, but here are the ones used in the projects in this book.

Canvas, corduroy, and denims are perfect for when you need a sturdy base. I love to use these for art collages, floor mats, purses, and bags. Canvas and denim are awesome because you can paint and embroider on them, and corduroy adds a plushy contrast when you need it.

- PRINTED COTTONS are my favorite, especially for newbie sewers. They are affordable, plentiful, and really make a basic project go a long way. Just remember to always buy more fabric than you need, because oftentimes it will sell out.

- EMBELLISHED FABRICS will serve as a sweet addition to your stash. These are materials that are prequilted, embroidered, stitched, or have beads, sequins, trims/ribbons, or even buttons on them. They will be priced higher than their nonembellished counterparts, but you can offset that by scouting out discounted bolts, clearance remnants, newspaper coupons, or in-store sales in order to snatch these up. Even a little bit will go a long way as trim, appliqués, or pockets.

- OTHERS. For beginners, stick with other oh-so-easy fabrics like muslin, felt, velvet, light suede, flannel, fleece, linen, and gabardine. And when you do feel like a sewing sophomore, dive into jersey, silk, and lace.

DESIGN YOUR OWN MATERIAL

Sure, there are thousands of patterns and prints to choose from, but sometimes you might want to invent something exclusive. Here are some of my favorite methods.

1. FAUX BATIK. Look in the fashion art section of the craft store for a color-resist product that comes in a squeeze tube. (I use Tulip's Color Block.) Lay your fabric out on a table and draw or paint on your design with the color-resist. Let the resist dry, and then dye your fabric. When it is time to rinse the fabric, the resist will wash off and leave the original color behind—thus creating a batik effect. Very cool!

> ### Stitch in Time
>
> When I was twelve, my mother was a Girl Scout leader, and we were earning our sewing badge. We were making aprons. When I had finished hand-stitching the hem, I announced that I was finished. I picked up the apron, and low and behold, my skirt came right up with it—I had sewn the apron to my skirt! With that embarrassment, I vowed that sewing was not for me. Forty years later, sewing is my therapy. I am still sewing, and loving it!
>
> —JEAN KULCSAR,
> Cuyahoga Falls, Ohio

2. DYE. Velvet, canvas, silk, muslin—any of these will look beautiful dyed. I'm addicted to ready-to-go types that are premixed in squeeze bottles. Simply wet your fabric, wring it out, and lay it flat. Add water to the bottle, shake, and then squirt it on. If you want defined edges of color, do not wet your fabric first. If you want a tie-dyed effect, simply scrunch your fabric and use rubber bands to hold the wadded-up fabric in place.

> ### *Stitch in* Time
>
> I love to listen to podcasts as I sew. I can plug in and listen to something fun, interesting, educational, or all of the above! When I found there weren't many about sewing, I started my own. It was really fun and easy, and I've met tons of wonderful listeners and fellow "sewist" enthusiasts.
>
> —MEGAN TELLIANO,
> Elk Grove, California

If you don't want to use store-bought dye, try going *au naturelle*. Start with 100 percent cotton or muslin. In a large pot, brew up about ten to twelve large tea bags. (Black tea works best.) Boil on high for ten minutes until it is very dark. Insert your fabric and let it soak for fifteen minutes. Use tongs or a chopstick to pull it out to check the color. The longer you leave it, the darker it will become. Carefully remove it and rinse it in the sink. Tumble dry and iron. Experiment with other natural dyes, such as green tea, blueberry tea, or even coffee or cranberries.

3. PAINT. Using lightweight muslin or silk, wet your fabric, wring it out, and lay it flat on a table. Use a wide brush and slightly watered down acrylics or fabric paint to add strokes of color. You could also try rubber or foam stamps. To create a blended look, squirt with a water bottle.

TIP: For a detailed paint job, stabilize your fabric by using a large embroidery hoop to keep it taut while you paint. You can also outline your designs or write words by using a permanent fabric marker.

4. METALLIC ACCENTS. Add dimension to printed fabrics with drawn-on dots, stars, swirls, and squiggles (I'm a softie for Jacquard's Neopaque).

5. STITCHED. Sew over plain fabric with contrasting-color thread, or embroidery floss.

6. MOSAIC. Sew fabric scraps together for a patchwork look.

7. BLEACH PEN. Add designs to boring fabric with a bleach pen. Simply add your design, let dry, and wash off.

8. GLITTER. Make your fabric sparkle by spraying it with permanent fabric glitter.

TIPS:
• When coloring fabric, make sure it does not have stain guard because the color will not set.
• Cover your work area with a large plastic garbage bag or newspaper.
• Prewash and dry fabric first.
• Always wear plastic gloves.

IMAGE TRANSFERS

We all have our favorite images, patterns, books, foreign newsprint, and album covers. Just look around your house or bedroom at your wall décor. Now you can take all those pictures you love and incorporate them into your work. It's important to know that many images are copyrighted—so you absolutely cannot sell them. However, you can use them for personal projects or gifts. So here's the skinny on how to take your favorite picture of Frida Kahlo and transfer it to a spiffy piece of cotton.

Fabric Sheets

You'll want to load up on these. This is a special chemical-coated fabric that is fused to a paper backing, and then cut to the standard size of copy paper. You then insert the sheet in a printer using either the copier, scanner, or printing function from your computer, and print away. Peel off the paper backing and sew. But there's more. Fabric paper comes in a variety of textures and colors, such as silk, cotton, black, and white. It also comes in a variety of applications—on a roll, peel-and-stick, iron-on, sew-on, and T-shirt transfers (make sure to print these backwards because when you use them, the image will come out in reverse). For the projects in this book, cotton sew-on fabric paper is all you need.

Once you have the fabric sheets, you must decide on how to apply the photo. There are two ways: toner-based or ink-jet. Toner photos are powder-based and the images are created by using black and white, or color, laser printers (found at your workplace or local copy center). I'm devoted to ink-jet transfers because they can be easily used with any home office printer/scanner/copier. The ink is wet and water-soluble and prints directly onto the fabric in a few minutes.

TIP: If you are going to use a photo on dark fabric, buy the specific fabric paper made for it.

HOW TO DO IT

1. Choose your photo and scan it into your computer.

2. Using photo software, adjust the image to your liking—resize it, add text, change the color, etc.

3. When you're ready to print, choose the high-resolution option because the ink soaks into the fabric and will come out a few shades lighter than what you see on your computer screen.

4. Following the directions in your printer's user manual, insert the fabric sheet and print the image.

5. Let it dry for a few minutes, and then cut and use it as desired.

Want to make your own fabric sheets? No problem. Simply use 100 percent cotton fabric and then soak it in a product called Bubble Jet Set, a chemical that allows the ink to transfer easily onto the fabric. You let it dry, iron the treated fabric to freezer paper, and cut it to the size of a piece of standard copy paper. It sounds like a lot of work, but it will save you money. If you plan to make lots of projects, you might want to consider this route. I prefer the ease of buying the sheets at the store. They are a teeny bit pricey, which is why I always look for store coupons in the newspaper or the mail.

DIY Appliqués

Once you have your image on fabric, you want to make it look nice and polished. I like to use the zigzag or satin stitch feature on my machine and sew all around the edge. You can also add a bit of brush-on glitter, or embroider accents to make the image even more glamorous. That way, when you sew or iron it on, it will look just like a professional artful appliqué! Another idea is to sew the fabric photo to a larger piece of contrasting fabric, so it will have a nice framed background.

> ### Stitch in Time
>
> When I was a little girl, my mother made all my clothes. She even made my dolls' clothes. At the time I resented it. I wanted store-bought, just like the other girls! But now I look back and think WOW! How did she do it? She worked full time and still made time to sew. Now that I am older and a busy mom too, I don't sew because I own a glue gun. I want to sew and I will! When I do, my first project will be window treatments for my bathroom!
>
> —TERRI OUELLETTE, Phoenix, TV personality, author, www.aterrioshow.com

TIP: I like to make all my appliqués as "iron-ons." To do that, I use Aleene's Liquid Fusible Web—this is a rubbery liquid that you brush on the back of your appliqué. Let it dry for twenty-four hours, and then it's ready to be ironed on! This is great for when you make your appliqués in advance. They are already turned into iron-on patches!

CRAFTY CHICA'S ARTFUL STITCHING 4–1–1

Close your eyes and imagine yourself in a field of flowing fabrics, satiny ribbons, and button-trimmed flowers. The scent of fresh linen permeates the air. You're sitting at a sewing machine, and spools of threads sing to you from the sky above. You drop in the bobbin, and smile, as it salutes you before you snap the case over it. You begin to feed yummy garnet silk through the presser foot and gasp in amazement because what comes out from the other side is golden and gorgeous! Yay! Sewing is easy and fun!

Stitch in Time

There are three words that I love to say. I use them when a friend points at something new that I am holding or wearing. I smile, my chin juts out just a couple of milli-meters, my chest puffs the tiniest bit, my answer has just a trace of pride, and I say my favorite three words . . . "I made it."

—AMY,
Sydney, Australia

OK—hold up right there . . .

We all have fantasies about the perfect sewing experience. (One time after sewing into the wee hours of the morning, I could have sworn I heard my spools of threads singing to me, too, but that's another story.) My ultimate goal? Low stress. That can be achieved by taking the time to educate and empower yourself. While it's great to just sit down and stitch, it helps to have a clue or two. Or three . . .

I know from experience. With my first machine, I tossed aside the user manual, figuring I could use my common sense. That led to a world of frustrations that I want to spare you from. That's why I've laid out all the nitty-gritty details. Take time to read through it all, so when you finally do sit down at your machine, you'll be a confident sewing warrior goddess!

KNOW THY MANUAL

These days, I keep a copy of the most important pages in my sewing machine's user manual in a plastic sleeve with my sewing supplies. Try it. It's handy for times when your mind goes blank or when you get stuck. You can print out a poster-size version and hang it up in your sewing area.

CREATE AN INSPIRATION BOOK

This is a notebook or journal where you can save ideas, tape in pictures, or keep your color swatches. If you don't want to keep it in a book, you can hang up a bulletin board and pin the goodies on.

BE CURIOUS

If you have friends who sew, grill them on their favorite machine and features. Ask them about mistakes they have made, or tips they learned. Watch a sewing show on TV. Visit a sewing or fabric store and check out the offerings. If you have time, take a class. All of this will help you to . . .

Stitch in Time

My first daughter was born three months premature. I was a teenage mother with very limited funds. She spent her first few weeks lying on a diaper struggling to survive. When the time came for me to hold her, I knew she needed a special dress. Because I had been sewing and selling doll clothes since I was fourteen, I pulled out a baby doll clothes pattern and sewed her very first baby gown—a long white dress scattered with red baby roses and a matching bonnet.

—SHARON MADSEN,
Lakeville, Minnesota

CHOOSE A MACHINE

There are two types: mechanical and electronic. Mechanical is what I started on, and I highly recommend it for newbies. I loved that it was simple and sturdy. I used every feature backwards and forwards and that built up my confidence. Basic machines have simple functions, all-rotary parts, a variety of stitches, and are reasonably priced (around $100). These machines are often on sale at discount department stores and have great mileage. However, I would stay away from the cutesy mini-machines, unless you only want to use them for small craft projects. Now, if you are semi-experienced and want to take your work to the next level, dive into the world of electronic machines. They are pricey ($500 and up), but worth it. Many come with an automatic threader, drop-in bobbin, oodles of fancy stitches, speed controls, and lots more. I used both types for the projects in this book. You can also visit a local sewing machine dealership and look for gently used models. If you don't have the cash to buy a new machine, ask family and friends if they have one to lend or give you.

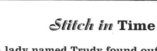
NAME AND DRESS UP YOUR MACHINE

Consider your sewing machine your new best friend. You two want to appreciate each other and work together to create fabulous, high-quality designs. Give her a name. Learn her quirks and how to make the most of them. Most important, decorate her with crystals, stickers, or rub-on letters!

THE BASICS

Sewing machines are like coffee drinks at Starbucks. There are those with fancy names, mini or extra-large sizes, exotic flavorings, extras like whipped cream and sprinkles. There are hardcore varieties, and old school simple models. But when it comes right down to it, all machines are basically the same—they all sew!

Definitely refer to your machine's user manual, but here's an easy breakdown of the features every machine has:

- ACCESSORY BOX AND EXTENSION TABLE: This is a removable portion of the machine that holds tools and bobbins.
- BOBBIN: A spool made of metal or plastic that holds the bobbin thread.
- BOBBIN CASE: This is the compartment that holds the bobbin in place within the machine.
- BOBBIN STOP: Located next to the winder, it moves to the left to hold the bobbin in place while the bobbin is being threaded.
- BOBBIN WINDER: This transfers the thread from the spool pin to the empty bobbin.
- FEED DOGS AND NEEDLE PLATE: This is a metal plate under the machine that has tiny teeth to grip the fabric. It works in tandem with the presser foot to happily guide your fabric through the sewing process.
- FLYWHEEL: The large, chunky wheel located on the upper right side. Turn it toward you to move the needle up and down as needed.

- FOOT PEDAL: Connects to the side of the machine. Step on it to set the needle in motion. The harder you press, the faster it goes.

- FREE ARM: Remove the extension table to use the free arm for working on tubular areas, such as cuffs, armholes, and the like.

- NEEDLE: Only the most important piece of this whole book!

- NEEDLE CLAMP AND SCREW: Holds the needle tightly in place. Unscrew it to remove the needle.

- PRESSER FOOT: This handy L-shaped foot holds the fabric in place while it's being fed through the machine. Always make sure to lower the presser foot before you sew.

- PRESSER FOOT LEVER: This moves up and down to raise and lower the presser foot.

- REVERSE STITCH LEVER: Used for backstitching (do this at the beginning and end of each seam to seal it off). Press this and the foot pedal at the same time to make the machine sew backwards.

- STITCH LENGTH DIAL: Determines the length of your stitches. I keep mine at 3mm, except when I use zigzag to make decorative borders—then I use 5mm or even 6mm. The shorter the stitch, the tighter it holds.

- STITCH SELECTOR: Determines which stitch design you'll be using.

- UPPER THREAD GUIDE: This is at the top and acts as a guide for either sewing or winding the bobbin evenly.

- TAKE-UP LEVER: A metal lever that holds the top thread just right for even stitches.

- THREAD TENSION DIAL: This controls how much thread goes into each stitch. It should be adjusted according to what type of fabric you're using. A setting of 3 or 4 will work for all the projects in this book.

FIND THE PERFECT SPOT

So you have your machine and you know the working parts. Now it's time to get in the zone. The perfect scenario would be to find a corner in your home to set up a work area that's always ready to go. If not, the kitchen table will work just fine.

Stitch in Time

Sewing Nerd! In high school I sewed all my own party dresses and even tackled a wedding gown for a family friend. Some kids thought of me as a sewing nerd and a few even made fun of me. I kept on stitching and I have the last laugh and stitch now.

—CATHIE FILIAN, Los Angeles, producer and cohost of Creative Juice, www.cathieandsteve.com

Make sure you have these elements:

- A sturdy table
- A comfy chair so you can sit up tall
- Good lighting
- Room to spread out your materials
- A wastebasket to toss out cut threads
- A sewing box (see below)
- A pincushion

MUST-HAVE SEWING SUPPLIES

In a perfect world, it would be nice to have every kind of sewing gadget ever invented. I've bought them all, but honestly, I have yet to use each one. To get started with basic sewing (and the projects in this book), here's all you really need:

- A COLORFUL SEWING BOX to hold all your prized goodies. I use a vintage Samsonite train case that I découpaged in vintage *Vogue* sewing patterns.
- HIGH-QUALITY THREADS in various colors, or at least black and white.
- Various-sized NEEDLES (and a case to hold them).
    - Hand-sewing needles: Buy a pack of assorted types!
    - Machine needles: Lightweight for thin, silky fabrics, medium for cottons, and heavy-duty for denims or canvas. For best results, change your needle often.
- A nice PAIR OF SCISSORS. Great for basic snips and cuts. These are to keep by your machine for cutting threads and excess fabric.
- PINKING SHEARS. These are about $20, but well worth it. Look for sales at the local fabric or craft store to pick up a pair. I use my pinking shears for cutting all my fabrics. It prevents fraying and adds a fun, textured edge to fabric art.
- SEAM RIPPER for removing boo-boos
- FLAT RULER for quick measuring
- CLOTH MEASURING TAPE for larger measurements
- PINS Standard dressmaker pins are just right, unless you want to get all fancy and use the pretty colored ones.
- PINCUSHION I always go with the old-school tomato cushion. In fact, I have several. Did you know the little chili on the end is filled with sand to sharpen your pins and needles? Just poke the pin in and out!

- CHALK for marking fabric
- IRON AND PRESSING CLOTH After you sew your seams, turn the fabric over, place a pressing cloth (hanky!) over the seam, and steam iron the flaps flat. Keep in mind that the amount of steam will vary from fabric to fabric. Pressing your seams will make your life so much easier when you continue to work, and your end project will look crisp.

LUXURY ITEMS

If you have the money to spare, these are super-helpful tools. I went years without using these, but when I finally bought them, I loved them!

- ROTARY CUTTER, SEWING RULER, AND MAT Great for cutting large portions of fabric, evenly and smoothly.
- DISAPPEARING INK PEN You can draw a design, sew over it, and the ink vanishes like magic!
- SEWING GAUGE Handy for marking hems and seam allowances.
- DRESS FORM You won't need one for the projects in this book, but if you move onto designing clothing, it's worth the splurge.

Now that everything is in place, it's time to move on to the actual mechanics of the machine. This is where people often get nervous, but there's really no reason to. As long as you follow the directions, all systems are go.

HOW TO WIND YOUR BOBBIN, LOAD IT, AND THEN THREAD YOUR MACHINE

Read your machine's user manual for the specifics, but here's a quick reference guide to peek at when in doubt. This is the part where I always do the sign of the cross and whisper nice things to my machine. If you are a starter stitcher, know that you can master this. Take a deep breath and chant: "I can do it. I can do it."

Ready? Here we go . . .

Wind Your Bobbin First

1. Place a spool of thread on the spool pin.

2. Guide the thread around the bobbin thread guide and insert the end of the thread into the hole in the bobbin, from the inside out. Pull up and hold that thread end.

3. Place the bobbin on the bobbin winder, move the bobbin stop to the left, and step on the foot pedal to wind it. Make sure the thread is wound within the bobbin and not below or above it. If that happens, stop, and repeat the process. The bobbin will wind automatically until it is full and even. You will know because the bobbin stop will snap back to the right. Remove the bobbin, and snip the thread.

TIPS TO AVOID BOBBIN HEADACHES:
• Always use bobbins that are in perfect shape, not warped, dented, or cracked.
• Never wind a bobbin that already has thread on it.
• Always use the same weight of thread in your bobbin as you're using for the top thread.

Now Load Your Bobbin (for a Mechanical Machine):

1. Remove the extension table and lift the flap, exposing the bobbin area. Remove the bobbin case.

2. Using your left hand, hold the bobbin case so the little protruding arm is facing you, and in the other hand hold the bobbin. You want the thread end to face away from you. Insert the bobbin in the case.

3. Pull the thread through the angled slot in the case until you feel it click and grip in place. Raise the little lever to lock the bobbin in place.

4. Insert the bobbin case in the machine, so the protruding arm fits in place. Push it until you feel it lock in place.

5. Close the little flap. Yippee! You did it!

Threading the Machine

1. Turn the flywheel to bring the needle up as high as it goes. Lift the presser foot.

2. Insert the thread on the spool pin so the end comes from behind. Take that end and feed it through the upper thread guide, down the front of the machine's front thread guide and then up and around the take-up lever going right to left.

3. Now draw the thread back down the same slot toward the needle. There will be a small guide above and behind the needle. Insert it in there and thread the end through the needle's eye, going front to back. Pull out an 8–10" (20.5–25.5cm) tail.

4. Pat yourself on the back—just one more step to go!

Bringing Up the Bobbin Thread

1. Hold the tail of the top thread semi-taut with your left hand in an upwards position.

2. Use your right hand to turn the flywheel one rotation toward you until the bobbin thread comes up and forms a loop.

3. Pull it up and out with your fingers.

4. Pull the top and bobbin threads out and under the presser foot and to the back 8–10" (20.5–25.5cm). If you cut them too short, your needle will unthread.

5. Congratulations—you're ready to sew!

HOW TO SEW

You didn't think I'd leave this part out, did you? That's why we're here!

1. Line up two pieces of fabric and insert pins horizontally.

2. Set your knobs. Stitch length: $\frac{1}{8}$" (3mm); straight stitch.

3. Lift the lever to raise the presser foot.

4. Place your fabric on the needle plate and line it up with the guide.

5. Turn the flywheel toward you until the needle goes into the fabric.

6. Lower the presser foot.

7. Slowly step on the pedal to make the machine start, go forward a few stitches, and stop. Make sure to remove each pin just before the needle reaches it. Press the reverse button and step again to backstitch. Stop and go forward to continue your seam.

8. When finished, backstitch, take your foot off the pedal, and turn the flywheel toward you to raise the needle. Lift the presser foot.

9. Slide out the fabric to the left, leaving an 8–10" (20.5–25.5cm) tail. Cut.

10. Cut excess thread from the fabric. Use an iron to press open the seam, if desired.

Practice Makes Perfect

You are probably super-stoked to start your first project. Hang on just a little bit longer. Take some time to practice and get to know your machine's functions. Take a piece of scrap fabric (a cotton dish towel or a hankie will work great, too) and practice straight stitches, curves, turns, zigzags, backstitching, and the like. Practice changing threads and bobbins. Save this piece of scrap fabric for use in a project later on!

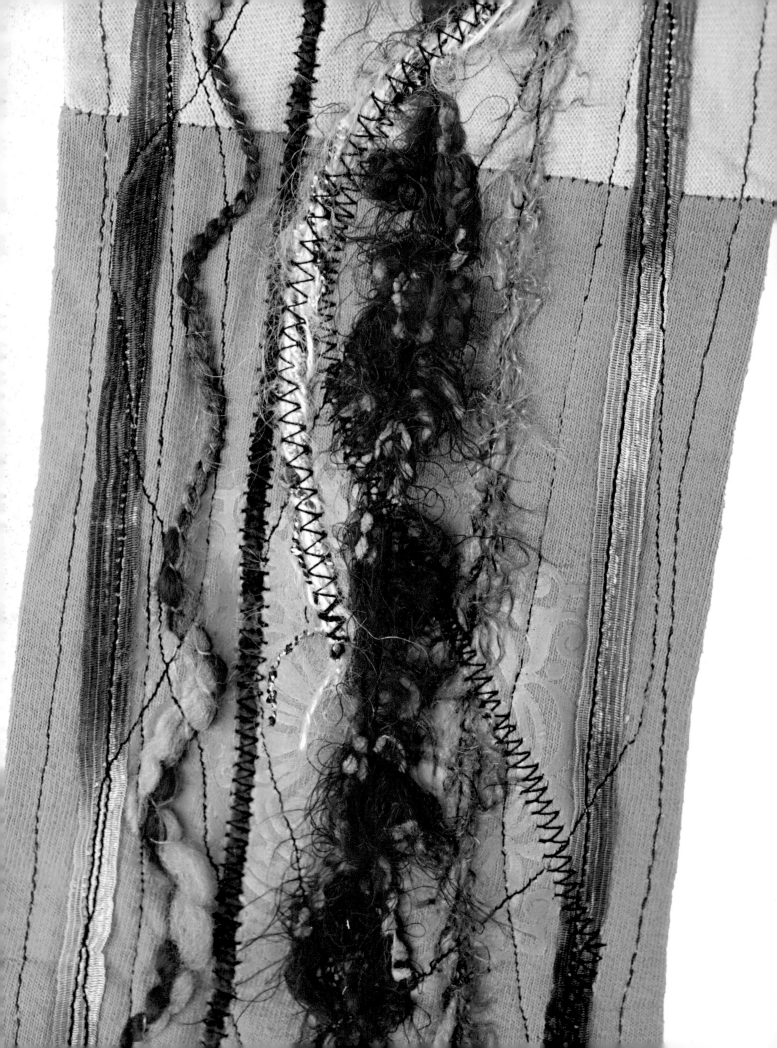

STITCHES

Be Edgy

Wondering what to do with those edges?
Well, there are lots of methods to indulge
in. Here are some simple ones to try.

- ROLLED HEM: Learn it. Use it.
  No one likes frayed edges, not even
  Edward Scissorhands. Not only will
  your work have everlasting life, but
  it will look spiffy too. First you want
  to cut the fabric with pinking shears.
  Fold the cut edge over about $\frac{1}{8}$"
  (3mm), and then again. Pin it in place
  and then sew up the center, using the
  straight stitch.

- ZIGZAG HEM: On some projects, you'll want to have a rough, artsy
  look and feel. But it's still OK to close off the edges of your fabric by
  using the zigzag function on your machine. This will prevent fraying
  and add a nice textured border to your work.

- BIAS TAPE, SEAM BINDING, OR TWILL TAPE: This is lightweight
  trim that you can use to finish off your edges. You simply fold it over
  your edge, pin, and sew it in place. Not only does it look tidy, but it
  also gives your work a nice, uniform look. For heavier projects, go with
  twill tape. It's a bit thicker, and thus sturdier.

- RICKRACK: Sometimes when I feel extra frilly, I'll use rickrack to
  finish off my edges. It's fun, and the curves make for an interesting look.

> ### Stitch in Time
>
> I've learned that almost
> anything can become fodder for
> sewing! If you see a curtain or
> a bed sheet or a shower
> curtain or even plastic bags
> that you like the color and look
> of—go for it. It might just
> become something fabulous
> and get you in the *New York
> Times*.
>
> —MELISSA FEHR,
> London (UK)

THREADS

Are all threads created equal? Not quite. They may look similar, but don't
let the pretty colors fool you. My favorite is 100 percent cotton, because
it's the strongest and most durable. Stay away from the dollar bin when it
comes to your spools. Stick with high-quality brands, such as Coats &
Clark or Gutermann. Cheap threads shed, and will wear down your
precious machine. However, polyester will work just fine. Rayon and silk
threads are gorgeous and tempting, but they break easily. I would save
these for decorative accents, and not for holding your pieces together.
Heavy-duty threads are must-haves for fabrics like duck cloth, canvas, or
denim, but make sure you have a heavy-duty needle to go with them.

INTERFACING

This is the miracle stuff that makes our collars and cuffs stiff. It also works wonders with fabric books and purses. It comes in various weights, ranging from light to heavy. It comes in single-sided fusible, double-sided fusible, or nonfusible. Oh. Let's explain fusible. That means it is coated with a layer of adhesive that can be ironed onto fabric.

BATTING

This is the fluffy stuff that quilters use in between their fabrics to create a puffy look. It's a great way to add dimension to your fabric collages. All it takes is a little pinch of batting between your layers to do the trick.

EMBELLISHMENTS

These are the rainbow sprinkles on your work. The simplest project can be taken over-the-top just with a little TLC from the accent department. Here are some ideas to add to your imagination menu:

- Charms, lockets, beads, pins
- Ribbons, fringe, sequin trim, iron-on crystals, appliqués
- Buttons, small chains, metal tags
- Embroidery, metallic threads, painted accents

IF NOTHING ELSE—REMEMBER THESE WORDS OF WISDOM

Always backstitch at the beginning and end of your seam. Back-stitching is when you sew in reverse and then forward. It prevents the stitches from opening.

Always double-check your measurements before (ack!) cutting your fabric or sewing.

If you're using patterned or printed fabric, always make sure you pinned it in the correct direction before you sew. And—make sure you are sewing on the correct side. My Nana Cano once sewed the back of my bridesmaid dress on inside out! All it takes is a quick peek to make sure. It will save you precious minutes (or, heaven forbid, hours).

Read the project directions from start to finish before you begin to make it.

Keep your pincushion nearby. While you are sewing, remove each pin before the needle hits it. Put them immediately in the pincushion;

otherwise, they can fall on the floor and poke your bare foot—or your cat's paw—when you least expect it.

If you're not sure about where to sew, use your machine's basting stitch. This is a loose, long stitch to help you see how things are going. If you like what you see, switch to your regular stitch. If not, make the correction as needed. Basting stitches are much easier (and faster) to remove than smaller stitches!

Remember that 36" (91cm) equals one yard.

Press your seams.

When sewing on buttons, always use double strands of thread so they will stay on forever!

> ### *Stitch in* Time
>
> One of my favorite projects was a messenger bag I made from several pairs of pants I had worn while I was volunteering. I didn't want to throw them away, because they reminded me of the whole life-changing experience and the community. But they were too old and ratty to wear. Making them into a useful bag, I was able to once again "wear" the pants, every paint splatter and stain a reminder of the work we did.
>
> —JULIANA RINCÓN,
> Medellín, Colombia

SEWING BY HAND

There are times when you should give your machine a rest and use your good ole hands and fingers to sew. What I love about hand-sewing is that you can use this tried-and-true method for so many reasons.

In fabric collage art. You can tack down your pieces before you take them to the machine.

For those tricky spots where a machine can't get to.

When your machine goes kaput and you have to finish your work *right now*.

Quick hem and/or button fixes.

Embroidery.

CRAFTY CINEMA

I love to watch movies while I sew, because it makes me feel like
I have friends around and I don't have to entertain them. Here's a list
of titles that have showcased sewing on the silver screen.

NACHO LIBRE (2006): Lucha libre costumes, masks, and a party suit all made in a church orphanage.

MYSTERY MEN (1999): Fashionista designer creates state-of-the-art superhero costumes.

KINKY BOOTS (2005): Boring shoe factory gets a drag queen makeover by way of boots.

THE INCREDIBLES (2004): Dysfunctional superhero costumes.

HOW TO MAKE AN AMERICAN QUILT (1995): Drama at the quilting group!

GONE WITH THE WIND (1939): Emergency dress made from drapes.

GANDHI (1982): One man inspires India to return to hand-spun materials.

ENCHANTED (2007): Day dresses made from drapes.

DICK (1999): Clothes made from the American flag.

THE COLOR PURPLE (1985): Woman empowers herself by designing trousers

THE NIGHTMARE BEFORE CHRISTMAS (1993): Rag doll Sally proves to be a whiz with the stitches.

PRETTY IN PINK (1986): Prom dress redo.

REAL WOMEN HAVE CURVES (2002): Drama at the sewing factory!

THE SOUND OF MUSIC (1965): Kids' play clothes made from drapes.

SPIDER-MAN (2002): Superhero suit made from pajamas.

TIM BURTON'S CORPSE BRIDE (2005): Wedding suit repaired with the help of spiders and their silky webbing.

WEST SIDE STORY (1961): Party dress alterations.

Here Are the Basics

1. Cut your thread to about 15–18"
(38–45.5cm).

2. Snip an end so it is clean and
fray-free.

3. Thread the end through the eye
of the needle.

4. Bring it down so the threads are even (yes, double it!).

5. Tie a double knot at the end.

Hand-Sewn Stitches

- BASTING STITCH: This is a longer version of the running stitch and is used to hold your fabric pieces together momentarily. Stitches should be about ½" (13mm) long.

- END STITCH: Make sure you have at least 3" (7.5cm) of thread left, and poke your needle through to the wrong side of the fabric, sew a loop, insert the needle through it and pull taut. Snip the excess. Confession: I've also tied the two ends together in a knot when I ran out of thread.

- RUNNING STITCH: This is when you weave in and out of the fabric. Your stitches will look like dashes and should be about $1/8$" (3mm) long.

- WHIPSTITCH: This is when you are in a hurry or don't want to mess with the running stitch, or when you want to look super arty and show off that fancy metallic thread. Simply sew your stitches, ¼" (6mm) up and down with an even diagonal slant.

FINALLY—SIGN YOUR WORK!

Each piece of fabric you sew will be created with care and creativity. Be proud of that and leave your mark on your work by making your own labels. As you work on your designs, sew a label inside your handbags, your garments, and furnishings. It's the sign of a true artist.

How to Do It

Insert a sheet of fabric paper in your printer. Use the address label feature on a computer design program to add your signature or company logo. Print it out, cut with pinking shears, or seam the edges with your zigzag function, and sew it on!

TIP: If you're using them on clothing that will be washed, ink-jet ink will run when water hits it, so use fabric markers to sign your name.

Stitch in Time

My best friend taught me how to sew by hand when we were about eight. We started with small bags, which were really just two square pieces of fabric. When we finished, the stitches were too big, so the "bags" wouldn't really hold anything. Frustrated, we reached for the glue and glued the sides together. The finished product was stiff and ugly, but I will never forget my first "lesson"!

—CHRISTIE MCNABB,
Anderson, Indiana

HOW TO USE A SEAM RIPPER

Removing stitches is always a last resort. And usually when you realize there is no other option, you're so frustrated that you just want to pull the thread out with your teeth! Take a deep breath and think of this as a learning experience. There is a right way and a wrong way to remove stitches with a seam ripper.

Our first instinct is to open the fabric ends and rip the thread up the center. Wrong. That will increase the chances of rips. The correct way is to leave the fabric flat and rip the seam from the side. Calm and peaceful. See? That wasn't so bad.

CRAFTY CHICA'S
~ode to~
SEWING

(every little bit helps!)

Oh great fabric maker in the sky
Please, oh please!
Surround my workspace with good vibes, patience, and creativity.

Guard these delicate fingertips from pinpricks and savage snips,
Whether by thimbles of steel or old-school divine intervention.
I don't care, I just need hardcore protection!

Structured or freeform,
Let my needle sew straight and sturdy for stitches big and small.
And allow my scissors to fly through fabric upon my call.

Sure, I can handle ripping a seam, or even losing my pincushion.
But you know where I really need the lucky charms?
Bobbins, patterns, and tension!

Silk, cotton, plastic, oilcloth.
Scarves, purses, journals, jackets.
I'm smart, savvy—and soon I'll be a superstar stitcher.

Just keep it cool and I'll follow through!

Chapter NO.

1

POWER PURSES

Next to chocolate and GLITTER,

designing and sewing purses have to be my all-time
favorite guilty pleasures. Purses are as functional as
they are fashionable—especially if they are *muy* eye-
catching and clever. I've made sure that each of these
handbags has a special Crafty Chica twist that will
spark some lively "Where did you get that?" conversa-
tion. If a nail-biting moment of self-doubt creeps up,
relax. Remember, the only way to conquer fear is to
think positively, have faith, use your skills and common
sense . . . and chant a prayer under your breath. On page
42 is a power prayer I came up with. Use it to inspire
you, or come up with your own prose. Hey! Print it out
on fabric paper and incorporate it into a project!

~ Thirsty ~
TOWEL TOTE

Ready to hit the beach? Save your change for sunscreen and flip-flops instead of using it for a new tote bag. Chances are you have a jumbo-sized beach towel in your house, just waiting to be transformed into a stylish terry-cloth purse. This project even has a bonus: Most beach towels are large enough to make more than one tote. Experiment, and see what you can come up with!

SKILL LEVEL Easy

MATERIALS

1 beach towel, 40" x 70" (101.5cm x 178cm), with wide trim

Pinking shears

Standard sewing machine needle

Matching thread

Straight pins

CRAFTY CHICA TIP

If you want to start with a brand-new towel, choose one that already has a trim and a cool appliqué design. It gives you a nice head start and will make your tote look ultra-polished!

~ HOW TO MAKE IT ~

1. Fold the towel lengthwise. With your pinking shears, cut the trim off one end of the towel and set it aside. This will be used to make the handles for the tote.

2. At the other end of the towel, keep the trim (this is the bottom of the bag), and use your pinking shears to cut 12" (30.5cm) up, as this is the top of the bag. Toss aside the excess. You won't need it.

3. Unfold the towel and seam the raw edge by using the zigzag function on your sewing machine to prevent fraying.

4. Now sew a rolled hem (see page 35).

5. Fold the towel again in the same fashion, right side out. Sew the sides, and at the bottom, just above the trim.

6. Take the trim you set aside earlier, and cut it in half so you have two straps. Seam the raw ends, using the zigzag function.

7. Pin the ends of each strap to the inside of the tote, making sure they are lined up evenly. Sew in place.

TIPS:

- To make secure handles, sew the strap by creating a square shape, and then an "X" inside the square.

- Use the extra towel to make smaller totes, or small hand towels.

- If you cannot find a towel with a pretty appliqué or trim, use iron-on patches, or embroider a design.

CRAFTY LIT

When you need a break from the pincushion, try curling up with a juicy novel that has sewing as the backdrop. It's a fun way to keep up your spirits, and maybe even pick up a few tricks and tips. Visit your local library or bookstore to find a wide array of quilting novels, and even a mystery series.

Super Elegante
MERCADO BAG

I'm a sucker for oversized Mexican tote bags that are sold at open-air markets (that's *mercado* in Spanish). The colors are so wild and bright, and the designs are simply striking. But I also adore oilcloth (laminated fabric). So what's a crafty chica to do? Merge the two! This roomy bag, which is all about contrast, is inspired by the vibrant displays of fruits and veggies at the market. But I'll bet this bag will be used for much more than just grocery shopping! This bag will measure 18" (45.5cm) across, 15" (38cm) tall and 7" (18cm) deep. Feel free to snip away any overage. The idea is to create a mosaic/patchwork type of bag that shows off all the happy colors of the oilcloth!

SKILL LEVEL Intermediate

MATERIALS

1 piece oilcloth, 8" x 36" (20.5cm x 91cm)

12 pieces contrasting oilcloth, 3½" x 3" each (9cm x 7.5cm)

6 pieces contrasting oilcloth, 2" x 6" each (5cm x 15cm)

8 pieces oilcloth, approximately 2" x 4" (5cm x 10cm)

2 pieces matching oilcloth, 7" x 19" each (18cm x 48.5cm)

Pinking shears

Straight pins

1 spool of bright red thread

Heavy-duty sewing machine needle

2 pieces of black seam binding, 2" x 32" each (5cm x 81cm)

NOTE Cut all oilcloth with pinking shears.

HOW TO MAKE IT

1. Pin and sew the 12 pieces of oilcloth together in sets of three (you will have four pieces).

2. Pin and sew the 6 pieces of oilcloth together in sets of three (you will have three pieces).

3. Now you will mix and match these sets to create two panels that measure 6" x 36" (15cm x 91cm) each. You can cut some in half and sew them to create a more interesting pattern, or just sew them as is, so both panels are equal in design style. Tip: Don't get intimidated by the measurements. All you're doing is creating two panels made from oilcloth scraps—each one needs to measure about 8" wide (20.5cm) and 36" (91cm) long.

4. Now you will have three long panels—two with patchwork-looking designs, and one with a single pattern. Pin and sew these three pieces together so they overlap. Use a variation of zigzag and straight stitch to add dimension.

5. Pin and sew together the 8 pieces measuring 2" x 4" (5cm x 10 cm) so you have two sets. Sew one on one end of the panel, and one on the other to make the top border of the bag.

6. Take the two pieces of remaining oilcloth and pin each one along the outside of the panel to make the sides. You'll have to fold the panel twice. Sew in place, first using straight stitch, and then again using the zigzag. This will make your bag extra sturdy!

7. Sew the handles in place on each side of the bag. To make them extra secure, sew them on by creating a square shape, and then an "X" inside the square.

TIP: Oilcloth can be kind of sticky, so pick up a bottle of Sewer's Aid and rub a bit under the presser foot, on the needle, and on the plate. This will help the fabric glide through with ease.

ᕲ Indian ᕲ
TAPESTRY TOTE

Anything sparkly and shiny—I'm so there. That's why I love the culture of India.
From the cheery colors to the shoulder-shimmying music to the campy Bollywood movies.
So when I came across this flashy table runner on eBay, I just had to have it. Problem?
I didn't have a table to use it on. I did the next best thing—I made it into a drawstring bag.
To complement the rich texture, I went with sequined corduroy to create the body,
and I love how it turned out!

SKILL LEVEL Intermediate

MATERIALS

1 Indian or other kind of textured
table runner, 36" x 9" (91cm x 23cm)

Black sequined corduroy, 36" x 10"
(91cm x 25.5cm)

Black thread

Standard machine needle

Straight pins

1 piece black cotton fabric,
12½" (32cm) round

1 piece black bias tape for the
drawstring, 70" x 1" (178cm x 2.5cm)

1 chopstick

Tape

ᕲ HOW TO MAKE IT ᕲ

1. Take the table runner and the black corduroy and line them up horizontally, right sides facing. Pin along the edge, and sew two rows of the straight stitch.

2. At the top of the corduroy, sew a rolled hem (see page 35). Fold the fabric over 1½" (3.8cm), and sew two rows of the straight stitch.

3. With the wrong side facing, pin and sew two rows of stitches up the side.

4. Pin the piece of circular black cotton fabric to the bottom. Pull it taut and pin. Sew it in place with two rows of straight stitches.

5. At the top of the bag, where the side seam is, snip a small hole on either side so you can feed the black bias tape through, forming the drawstring.

6. Tape the drawstring to the end of the chopstick and insert it through the hole. Scrunch the corduroy until the chopstick comes out through the other hole.

7. Remove the drawstring from the chopstick and tie a knot at the end.

Stitch in Time

I remember as a kid first learning how to use the sewing machine. Frequently I tried to sew in zippers without using the zipper foot. Call me lazy—I can take it. I don't recommend taking this route. The zipper foot is there for a reason. Use it. Love it. Embrace it.

—WENDY RUSSELL, Vancouver, Canada, host of HGTV Canada's *She's Crafty*

"My Life Is an Adventure" POCKET BAG

A big part of being creative is appreciating your surroundings—stopping to smell the flowers, as we always hear. This project isn't only about smelling the flowers—it's about picking them and taking them with you. This purse, made from slide protector pages, is the perfect way to celebrate all your day's adventures. Every time you come across something that engages you, take a small memento to put in the purse's pocket. At the end of the day, look at it all to find that you truly lead an eventful existence. Another option? Slip in all your favorite pictures. Anything to keep you smiling!

SKILL LEVEL Easy

MATERIALS

Sewer's Aid

4 slide protector pages cut as follows (make sure to cut off the side flaps from each page):

2 pieces, 8½" x 11" (21.5cm x 28cm)

2 pieces, 4" x 11" (10cm x 28cm)

1 piece, 8½" x 4½" (21.5cm x 11.5cm)

2 pieces for the handles, 2" x 16" (5cm x 40.5cm)

Black thread

Heavy-duty sewing needle

Mini-pictures or mementos

HOW TO MAKE IT

1. Rub the Sewer's Aid on the needle, the plate, and under the presser foot.

2. You will not be able to pin because the holes will show through the plastic. Take one of the large slide protector pages, line it up with a side piece, and sew them together using the straight stitch.

3. Continue until all four sides are joined. Line up the bottom and sew it in place.

4. For the handles, take each strip and fold it lengthwise so it measures 1" (2.5cm) wide. Sew each handle in place on each side of the bag. To make them extra secure, sew them on by creating a square shape, and then an "X" inside the square.

5. Insert your goodies into the pockets!

TOTALLY TOTE-ABLE!

Canvas totes multiply like bunnies. Or at least it seems as if they do. From conferences, workshops, bookstores, and school—we all have a stack of bland bags in our closets. They are too sturdy and useful to toss out, but they hardly reflect our vibrant personalities. What's a crafty chica to do? Give them a makeover, of course! Here are some easy ways to make those totes go from tired to tantalizing!

- Cover up the boring logo by painting over it or sewing on colorful fabric to cover it.

- Cover it with all kinds of fabric patches, trims, or lace.

- Cut off the handles and sew on a long strap, so you can sling it over your shoulder to carry art supplies.

- Measure the width and height of the tote, and create a fabric collage to match. Sew the collage to a heavy fabric, like cotton, to give it substance. Now sew it to the top edge of one side of the tote bag to make a "flap" that hangs over the logo design.

- Flip the entire bag inside out and add trim around the top, and sides so the seams don't show.

All Work and All Play LAPTOP SLEEVE

Sometimes you're in a sock-monkey kind of mood, and sometimes you're not. It's the same thing with your laptop. There are times when you want to surf the latest celebrity gossip blogs, and other times when you just need to dive in and get your work finished. Either way, you're covered with this reversible laptop sleeve. Use it to protect your precious cargo from scratches inside your suitcase, briefcase, or purse. Use your favorite kitschy fabric on one side (Yay, sock monkeys!) and a pretty, professional print on another. When you're at the coffee shop surfing the Web, use the fun side. But when you're lunching with your boss and want to appear professional, simply flip it around. And there you have it—one attractive, functional laptop cover that is totally you!

SKILL LEVEL Intermediate

MATERIALS

1 yd (91cm) playful-looking fabric in your favorite theme

1 yd (91cm) fabric that is more sophisticated

1 roll batting

Straight pins

2 strands ribbon, 12" (30.5cm) long

2 small buttons

Sewing machine (or needle and thread)

HOW TO MAKE IT

1. Measure your laptop and add 2" (5cm) to the width, and triple the length. For example, if your laptop is 11" x 9" (28cm x 23cm), cut two pieces of each fabric measuring 13" x 27" (33cm x 68.5cm) each.

2. Cut a piece of batting 2" (5cm) smaller than your laptop's dimensions on all sides.

3. Lay one piece of fabric facedown, set down the batting on top of it, and then lay the other piece of fabric faceup, so it is like a sandwich. Start at one end, and carefully fold in the edges along the side, pinning in place. Do this on all four sides. Sew in place along the edge, so there is a nice, clean hem.

4. Sew all around the fabric so the batting will stay in place. Tip: If your pattern has squares or other simple shapes, you can use those as a guide; otherwise, feed the fabric through your machine in loops, swirls, or other appealing designs. Cut off loose threads.

5. Set the fabric lengthwise in front of you. Lift up the bottom end to create the "sleeve" portion. Use your laptop as a guide for how high to bring the end up. Pin the sides and sew them in place.

6. Close the top flap, measure 1" (2.5cm) down and hand-sew on a button to the body area of the sleeve. At the bottom of the front of the flap, fold the ribbon in half and, using needle and thread, tack it in place. This is to secure the flap closed—just wrap the ribbon around the button.

7. Turn the sleeve inside out and repeat step 6.

TIPS:

- If you're using patterned fabric with words or characters, you'll have to create three fabric "sandwiches" and sew them together so the pattern is right side up.

- For the closure, instead of a button and a ribbon, you can use Velcro or a small clasp. For greater contrast, use two kinds of fabric.

- Super-easy method: Use a pillowcase! Simply insert a layer of batting inside, and sew the top closed. Follow the remainder of the directions.

"I Will Never Part with This T-Shirt" GLITTER TOTE

I'm a big girl. And I used to get über-bummed when I'd find a cute T-shirt with the perfect sassy slogan—but not in my size. Sure I could complain, whine, and throw a hissy fit, but I'd much rather buy the shirt and whack it up to my liking. It's all about finding the joy, right? This project is also a happy solution when a shirt no longer fits, if it wears out, or if you just don't have an occasion to wear it anymore. Just cut out the design and transform it into a carryall tote, perfect for picnics, workshops, grocery shopping, or the gym.

SKILL LEVEL Easy

MATERIALS

1 canvas tote, 15" x 18" x 6"
(38 cm x 45.5 cm x 15 cm)

1 piece fabric, 15" x 18" x 6"
(38cm x 45.5cm x 15cm)

Pinking shears

1 T-shirt with a slogan/design you love

Heavy-duty fusible webbing

Pressing cloth

1 canvas tote, 15" x 18" x 6" (38cm x
45.5cm x 15cm)

Small paintbrush

Aleene's Glitter & Gem Glue

Microfine loose glitter

HOW TO MAKE IT

1. Create a curvy border by cutting the edges of the fabric with the pinking shears all the way around.

2. Cut out the design of the T-shirt in the same fashion, leaving a 1" (2.5cm) border around it.

3. Pin the T-shirt design to the center of the fabric and use the zigzag function to sew it together.

4. Open the fusible webbing, and smooth it out on a flat surface. Lay down your piece of fabric and cut the webbing to match it.

5. Take it to the ironing board and place the pressing cloth over the fabric. With the iron on high (no steam), affix the backside of the fabric to the sticky side of the webbing. Tip: Only iron to the edge of the fabric, so you won't get the webbing on your iron or pressing cloth. Let it cool, and peel off paper backing.

6. Now iron the fabric to one side of the tote.

7. To add contrast color to the handles, run them under the machine using the zigzag function.

8. Let's add glitter! Use the paintbrush to paint on the glue over the areas where you want the glitter. Sprinkle it on while the glue is wet, and tap away excess.

TIPS:

- Decorate the other side as well!

- If you really want to revamp your tote, cut off the handles and sew on new ones that you like better.

- Dye your tote before adding the fabric.

- For a puffy look, add batting in between the fabric and the T-shirt design and sew in the outlines.

Stitch in Time

In first grade, everyone in class was given a square foot (0.9m2) of burlap, colored yarn and a needle. The object: Stitch a self-portrait. We were to draw our body outlines in marker and then fill it with neat, orderly stitches. By the time I finished, my project looked exactly like me—if I had been Frankenstein's Amoeba. While other kids stitched in neat rows, my blob was filled with stitches that crossed and overlapped, bulging in the center from far too much yarn. Since then, I have sewed only once more—to attach a button when I tried to be self-stitching-reliant in my freshman year at college. By the time I was done, you could not see the button through the thread. But it stayed on. Success!

—SCOTT CRAVEN, Phoenix,
loseroldguy.com

Favorite Things Fabric
COLLAGE MESSENGER BAG

Ever wish you could buy a one-of-a-kind, custom-made designer handbag that has all your favorite themes on it? Here's your chance! And the best part is that you are the designer. This bag is *muy grande,* and is made for a day of power shopping. I love to take this bag to the park or a coffee shop and write in my journal. It's roomy enough to hold notebooks, a journal, a sketchpad, even a small laptop!

SKILL LEVEL Intermediate to Difficult

MATERIALS

Heavy cotton black fabric, 4 yd (3.6m), cut into the following pieces:

5 pieces (front and back panels' front flap), 15" x 12" (38cm x 30.5cm): Fabric A

6 pieces (side and bottom panels), 12" x 4" (30.5cm x 10cm): Fabric B

1 piece (strap), 36" x 6" (91cm x 15cm): Fabric B

Straight pins

Black thread

4 fabric images, sewn to contrasting background fabrics, each measuring approximately 5–6" (12.5–15cm)

3 types glittered, embroidered ribbon, 24" (61cm) each

1 piece gold fringe, 15" (38cm)

HOW TO MAKE IT

BODY OF THE BAG

First you want to construct the body of the bag. You are going to make two identical bags because one of them will serve as the lining. This will make it sturdy enough to hold heavy items.

TIP: When sewing the seams, first seam the edges using the zigzag function, and then sew straight stitch next to it.

1. Take one piece of fabric A and one 12" x 4" (30.5cm x 10cm) piece of fabric B and pin them together on one of the short sides. Pin a piece of fabric A to the end, so you have two fabric A pieces and one 12" x 4" (30.5cm x 10cm) fabric B piece in one long, horizontal piece. Sew.

2. Now join the pieces, by lining up the ends (wrong side out) and sewing.

3. You now have the shell of your bag, but it needs a bottom. Pin a 12" x 4" (30.5cm x 10cm) fabric B piece along the bottom edges (wrong side out), and sew it in place.

4. Repeat with the remaining pieces, so you have two bags.

5. Insert one of the bags inside the other, to serve as the lining. At the top, you will have two raw edges. Fold those in about ⅛" (3mm) and pin. Sew them in place using the straight stitch.

6. To make the strap, take the long fabric B strip, and fold it in thirds, lengthwise. Sew up the sides to hold it in place.

7. Pin one end 2" (5cm) down to the inner side of the bag, and sew a box and an "X." Repeat for the other side.

Stitch in Time

Do not sew while you're tired. You'll definitely regret it. Some past mistakes I've made as a result of burning the midnight oil: sewing the entire hem of a skirt without thread in the needle because I didn't notice that it had slipped out; stitching a pair of pants seams side-to-side instead of front-to-back; and my favorite, sewing the sleeve of the sweater I was wearing to the bag I was working on. I suppose the advice could also be "Do not wear long drapey sleeves while sewing."

—ALEX LANCETTE, Eau Claire, Wisconsin
(Una Luna on Etsy.com)

FRONT FLAP

8. Use a table to lay out the last piece of fabric A. Sew a rolled hem (see page 35) around the edges.

9. Set down your fabric images and arrange them to your liking on the fabric. Once you come up with a layout you like, pin the pieces together and sew them so you have one fabric collage.

10. Now sew that collage onto the last piece of fabric A. Sew on any other embellishments you want, including the ribbon and the fringe trim.

11. To attach the flap, line it up, wrong side out, to the back of the bag. Pin along the edge, and flip the flap over to ensure that everything looks right. Sew it in place, using two rows of straight stitching.

TIPS:

- If you don't want to construct the whole bag, simply use a ready-made canvas tote as the body of the bag and just cut off the handles.

- Add pockets to your bag. Sew a hemmed block of fabric to one of your bags before you sew in the lining.

~ Super Sweet ~
PLACE MAT PURSE

When I received my first sewing machine, I knew I wanted to start my stitched-filled journey with an easy project that I would be proud of. You can't get much easier than place mat purses! I visited a global-themed department store and picked up some cloth place mats that were lined and fully hemmed. Seam up the sides, and there you go—you just made a purse! If you're a beginner, projects like this are a surefire way to build your confidence because you'll always end up with something to brag about!

SKILL LEVEL Super-Easy	Matching thread	Set of purse handles
MATERIALS	2 yd (1.8m) of colorful trim for borders	Sewing needle
1 heavy-duty lined place mat	Straight pins	Charms or fringe (optional)

~ HOW TO MAKE IT ~

1. Fold the place mat in half (widthwise, right side out) and sew up each side.

2. Pin the trim along the top of the bag, and sew it in place.

3. Inside the purse, line up the handles at the top on either side of the purse. Use the sewing needle and thread to tack them in place so you know where to stitch them. This is to ensure that you sew them on evenly. Now stitch them securely in place.

TIPS:

- To add a shoulder strap, sew one end of a strip of wide trim to each side.

- To add more flair, hand-sew charms or add a row of fringe to the bottom.

- Buy several place mats and sew them together to make one large bag.

- You can also fold the place mat into thirds and add a clasp to make a clutch.

INTERESTING _tidbits_ ABOUT SEWING

While you're working away on your projects, here is some food for thought when it comes to the world of bobbins, thread, and needles.

- **HAND-SEWING** is ultra, ultra old school. It dates back twenty thousand years!

- The first **SEWING NEEDLES** were not what they are today. They were created from bones or animal horns. Later, in the fourteenth century, they morphed into iron needles. Oh, and the eye? That didn't come along until the fifteenth century.

- The **FIRST SEWING MACHINE** was created in 1830 by a French tailor named Barthelemy Thimonnier. The first successful American machine popped up in 1834, the brainchild of Walter Hunt. But in 1846, the first American patent went to Elias Howe. Isaac Singer built the first commercially successful machine in 1850, and the rest is history!

- Ever wonder what the difference is between **NETTING** and **TULLE**? Netting has bigger holes.

- The word **DENIM** comes from the French term _serge de Nimes_. It was a sturdy fabric made by the Andre Family. The name was ultimately shortened.

- Ellen Curtis Demores created the **FIRST PAPER SEWING PATTERNS** in 1860 for fashion magazines. Her business closed its doors in 1887, but a tailor named Ebeneezer Butterick launched his line in 1863.

- Can't find your measuring tape? The distance from your **NOSE TO YOUR FINGERTIPS** pretty much equals a yard (91cm).

- The oldest known **QUILT** is thought to have come from Egypt.

- 80 percent of the world's **ZIPPERS** are manufactured in a factory in Zhejiang Province, China.

- People who collect **THIMBLES** are called digitabulists.

~ Calaca ~
CLUTCH

This handy little wristlet celebrates *Dia de los Muertos*—Day of the Dead. That's a three-thousand-year-old Mexican tradition that celebrates the lives of our loved ones who have passed away. It involves mucho smiling skeletons, also known as *calacas*. This design is inspired by the Mexican sugar skulls that are prepared for the event. They are decorated with bright icing to represent the sweetness of life; the skull reminds us that while their body is no longer here, their spirit still is.

SKILL LEVEL Easy

MATERIALS

Templates from pages 129 and 130

2 sheets white craft felt

I sheet craft felt in each of the following colors: red, green, black, purple

Day of the Dead fabric, ½ yd (45.5cm)

Needle and thread

Yellow button

Black embroidery thread (optional)

Hot pink trim, ½ yd (45.5cm)

Fabric glitter or crystals (optional)

~ HOW TO MAKE IT ~

1. Make a copy of the templates. Cut them out. Using the photo as a guide, lay them on the corresponding felt colors and cut them out.

2. Make sure to cut two skull shapes out of both the white craft felt and the Day of the Dead fabric.

3. Take one piece of the skull shape, pin on the eyes, and then sew them in place. Continue with the remaining pieces of the face, the leaves, the cheeks, the heart, and the yellow button inside the heart.

4. To make the teeth, use a fun stitch pattern from your machine, or you can hand-sew them, using black embroidery thread. Another option is to sew on black squares of felt.

5. Turn on your machine's zigzag feature. With both fabrics right side out, sew the Day of the Dead fabric to each side of the skull shape, to serve as the lining.

6. Sew up the sides, stopping 2" (5cm) from the top.

7. Pin the hot pink trim around the front edge of the skull, and sew it in place. Remember to fold down the back flap as you sew toward the top.

8. Cut an 8" x ½" (20.5cm x 13mm) piece of black felt. Fold it and sew one end to the inside of each flap of the skull.

TIPS:

- If you don't want to use felt, use sturdy cotton fabrics.
- Play around with drawing your own shapes.
- Add fabric glitter or crystals if you want your bag to sparkle.

Stitch in Time

Years ago when I was making a purse out of a pair of children's training panties for an episode of *Stylelicious,* I had to call my mom for help. I had borrowed my sister's sewing machine, but for some reason threading the bobbin was the bane of my existence. I called Mom, hoping she could talk me through threading the bobbin over the phone. She tried her best to talk me through the steps like a bomb negotiator handling a hostage situation, but my bobbin still didn't have thread. I needed a pictorial guide. Mom resorted to going to her computer and scanning in her hands threading a bobbin step-by-step and e-mailed me the pictures. I finally figured out how to thread my bobbin and was off making panties into a purse!

—JENNIFER PERKINS, Austin, Texas, jewelry designer, TV personality, author, www.naughtysecretaryclub.com

Magnificent Milagro
CHARM POUCH

Milagros (miracles) are little charms from Mexico that are believed to bring you happiness, health, and love. They come in hundreds of different shapes, corresponding to areas where you need a little divine intervention. My Nana switches them out every week on a safety pin and attaches them inside her bra. When we go to church, she waves over the priest, and as he walks over, she quickly whips off the pin with her *milagros* from inside her bra so he can bless them. My Nana is the ultimate cutie and can get away with that. I, however, would probably get kicked out for that stunt. So I made this sweet charm pouch that is decorated with my favorite type of *milagros*—hearts!

SKILL LEVEL Intermediate

MATERIALS

2 pieces silky sequined fabric, 6½" x 10" (16.5cm x 25.5cm)

Straight pins

Lightweight sewing machine needle

Chopstick

Tape

2 pieces ribbon, 20" (51cm) long

12–15 Mexican milagros

Needle and thread

HOW TO MAKE IT

(DIAGRAMS ON PAGE 66)

1. Lay the fabric pieces together, wrong side out. Pin and sew up two long sides, and one short side (Diagram 1).

2. Turn the piece inside out, so right sides of fabric are facing out (Diagram 2).

3. Fold the raw edges inward, pin, and sew (Diagram 3).

4. At the same end, fold the corner under on both sides, and then fold the fabric inward about 1" (2.5cm). Pin and sew—but do not sew over the holes you created when you folded over the corners. This is the "tunnel" where the ribbon will be threaded through. Repeat this step for the other end (Diagram 4).

5. Fold the fabric in half widthwise, with the tunnels facing outward.

6. Pin and sew up the sides, stopping right before the tunnels (Diagram 5).

7. Turn the pouch inside out.

8. Take the chopstick and tape one of the pieces of ribbon to it. Thread it through the tunnel going right. When it comes out on the other side, remove the ribbon from the chopstick.

9. Repeat step 8, but this time thread the ribbon through the tunnel going left.

10. You will have strands coming out of both sides of the top. Tie a milagro onto each end.

11. Use the needle and thread to attach milagros all over the front and back of the pouch (Diagram 6).

12. Pull the strands, and there you have it—a pouch of miracles!

TIPS:

- Silky fabric can be a bit tricky. You can use velvet if you prefer.
- Instead of the milagros, you can attach beads or other charms.
- Use your pouch to hold special items, or use it to hold a small gift.

Stitch in Time

When my boys were kids, I bought cheap blankets and encased them in cute Peanuts character sheets. They weren't done artfully or neatly, but they did the job, and the boys loved the quilts. My boys are now grown men, and still use them faithfully. My advice is to be careful with any home sewing projects. You never know what oddity will become a family heirloom!

—KAY BUTLER, Phoenix

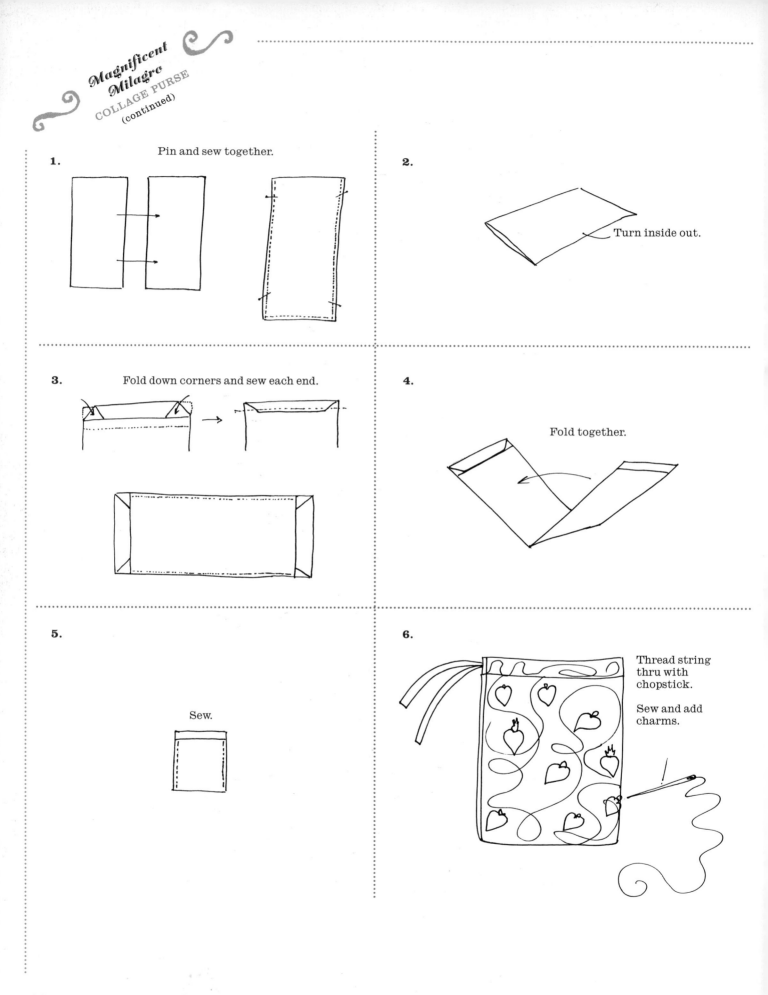

1. Pin and sew together.

2. Turn inside out.

3. Fold down corners and sew each end.

4. Fold together.

5. Sew.

6. Thread string thru with chopstick.

Sew and add charms.

2
WONDROUS WEARABLES

Before I began **SKETCHING IDEAS** for this book, I never thought of myself as a fashion designer. I was content with staying with my vast comfort zone of handbags, pillows, journals, and jewelry. But life is about pushing yourself up to the next level, even more so with art. So I flung myself into fashion! The best tip I can give is to tell yourself, "This is just for fun. No one is judging me." Buy some cheap clothing items from the thrift store, cut them up, and put them back together. Savor the design process. The following ten projects are great warm-ups and quite inventive—the perfect recipe for customizing your tired clothes, or adding personality to brand-new ones.

Reverse Appliqué
PARTY DRESS

The best outfits are those that have been tailored just for you. But not everyone can afford a personal seamstress or stylist. Therefore, I give you permission to take matters into your own hands and cut up that brand-new party dress! I'm not talkin' an expensive designer red-carpet number, but something more low key. Look for a basic strapless dress in a solid color. Consider it an empty canvas on which to work your magic with this simple reverse appliqué technique. It can also be used on jeans, bags, hats—just about anything!

SKILL LEVEL Intermediate

MATERIALS

Templates from pages 131 and 132

1/8 yd (11.5cm) cotton fabric in each of three colors: 1 piece red, 1 piece green, 1 piece yellow

Straight pins

1 solid-color strapless dress, preferably cotton

Contrasting colors of bobbin thread

Mini-scissors

3–4 yd (2.75–3.6m) lace or rickrack (depends on the size of the dress)

HOW TO MAKE IT

(DIAGRAMS ON PAGE 72)

1. Make a copy of the templates. Cut them out. Trace around the shapes onto the red, green, and yellow fabric. Cut out the shapes.

2. Turn the dress inside out and position the fabric pieces where you want them (Diagram 1). Pin and sew around the edges. Remove the pins.

3. Turn the dress right side out and use the mini-scissors to cut along the inside of the stitches so the fabric from underneath shows through (Diagram 2).

4. Pin and sew the trim all along the bottom of the dress, as well as the top (Diagram 3).

TIPS:

- Always play around with the placement of the fabric pieces before you sew them. Make sure you are 100 percent happy with where they are.

- Instead of the flower pattern, draw your own pattern. You can spell out words or create a geometric border along the bottom of the dress.

- Print your own painting or collage art onto fabric paper, peel off the backing, and use that as the fabric underneath.

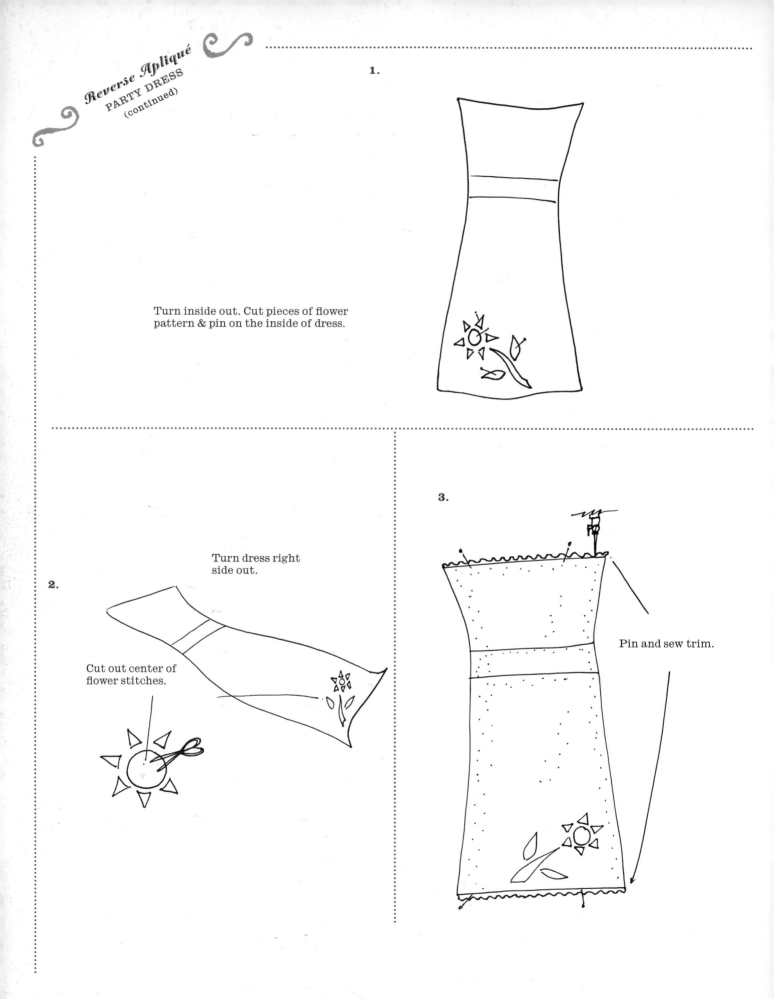

1.

Turn inside out. Cut pieces of flower pattern & pin on the inside of dress.

2.

Turn dress right side out.

Cut out center of flower stitches.

3.

Pin and sew trim.

Azul con Café
DIAMOND COLLAGE TANK

Tank tops are pretty much easy-come-easy-go. Maybe it's time we give them a double take. They are sexy, versatile, and timeless. And that's without any embellishments. This design takes the ordinary tank and gives it an artsy makeover.

SKILL LEVEL Easy

MATERIALS

1 dark brown T-shirt with a silkscreened design

Lightweight fusible fabric webbing

1 teal tank

Pressing cloth

Contrasting color thread

Sewing needle

3 white rose buttons

Thin liner brush

Permanent fabric adhesive

Washable micro glitter (polyester-based)

HOW TO MAKE IT

1. Cut seven 3" x 3" (7.5cm x 7.5cm) squares out from the silkscreen design from the brown shirt.

2. Apply the fusible webbing to the back of them (see page 55).

3. Place them on the tank in this order and iron them on one by one, using a pressing cloth:
   - Four down the left side, with the top points overlapping.
   - One in the center.
   - Two on the right side.

4. Sew the squares on the left side first, using the straight stitch.

5. Now sew on the remaining three squares, using the zigzag stitch.

6. Use a sewing needle and thread to stitch on three rose buttons in a row on the top right strap.

7. Use the liner brush and fabric adhesive to coat areas where you want glitter. Pour the glitter over the wet glue and tap away excess. Let dry.

TIPS:

- Instead of a silkscreen image, print your artwork onto fabric paper (see page 20). Here's a thought: Use vintage international postage stamps.

- If you don't have lightweight fusible webbing, you can still sew on the squares. Just make sure to pin and sew them very carefully, because jersey fabric can be very tricky!

- Use any kind of shapes. Long rectangles (as shown in photo), bouncy circles, or hearts, too!

 EASY WAYS TO *revamp* YOUR EXISTING CLOTHES OR ADD SOME *pop* TO BRAND-NEW ONES

- Use **TRIMS, RIBBONS, AND YARNS** to accent sleeves, collars, and hems.
- Chop your T-shirts horizontally into thirds, **MIX THEM UP**, and then sew them back together.
- Paint, felt a design, or sew an **APPLIQUÉ** at the top of the back of your jeans.
- Add **CONTRAST STITCHING** around the seams and hems of your clothes.
- Make use of **LINENS, NAPKINS, SHEETS,** and **DISH TOWELS** to use as fabric for your clothing alterations.

- Add **SPARKLE** to bland slogan T-shirts with iron-on crystals, gems, or sequins.
- **EMBROIDER** your name or a favorite phrase on a jeans skirt, jacket, hat, or even shoes.
- Cut long sleeves into short sleeves. And then use those sleeves to make short sleeves long on another top.
- Sew a **CASING** along the bottom of a shirt or blouse and add a **DRAWSTRING** to give the piece some dimension.

Yarn and T-Shirt SKINNY SCARF

After snipping out all those cool images from your shirts to make projects—it seems like a shame to ditch the leftover jersey. Same goes for leftover yarn remnants. In *el mundo de la Crafty Chica*, every little scrap has a place and a purpose. Watch and learn.

SKILL LEVEL Easy

MATERIALS

24 squares of leftover T-shirt, each one measuring 5" x 8" (12.5 x 20.5cm)

15–18 pieces of various contrasting color yarns, each one measuring about 5½ yd (5m)

HOW TO MAKE IT

1. Sort the fabric pieces into two sets of 12.

2. Start with one set, and sew the pieces together, right side in, so you have one long piece. Repeat with the other set of 12.

3. Line up the two long pieces and face them right side in. Sew around the edges on three sides, leaving a ⅛" (3mm) seam allowance.

4. Turn the scarf right side out. You don't have to sew up the open end.

5. Leaving a ⅛" (3mm) seam allowance, sew all around the edge of the scarf.

6. Use your scissors to snip the ends into fringe, about 7" (18cm) worth.

7. Sew half the yarn pieces on one side of the scarf—make sure to allow 7" (18cm) to hang over with the fringe. You can sew the yarn on the fabric in straight lines, or in curves, swirls, squares—whatever.

TIPS:

- For a more uniform look, use the same colors of fabric and yarn, or use only two colors, like black and white.
- To add sparkle, use yarn that has metallic thread in it.
- For even more texture, stitch up and down the scarf, using only thread.
- This is a good time to make use of all those stitch patterns you've always wanted to use!
- It doesn't matter if you make a few small mistakes; this design hides a multitude of sins!

Stitch in Time

If there is one tip I seriously stand by, it's that gold thread is bomb for hiding blunders by a new sewer. Even if the stitch is wrong, gold-threaded mistakes still look pretty!

—YOLI MANZO, Sacramento, California, Sacred Snatch Designs, www.myspace.com/sacredsnatch

Flouncy CROPPED COAT

Scarves and coats go together like peanut butter and jelly. Champagne and pearls. Regis and Kelly. But how about mixing up the formula, and literally combining the two into one super-fantastico piece of wearable art? Snipping and stitching have never been more eventful. Or toasty.

SKILL LEVEL Intermediate to Difficult	Fabric marking pen	I extra-long cotton/rayon scarf
	Measuring tape	Straight pins
MATERIALS	Pinking shears	2 yd (1.8m) rickrack
I cotton coat		

HOW TO MAKE IT

1. Put on the coat and hold one arm down at your side. Use a fabric marking pen to draw a small line about 2" (5cm) below your elbow. Repeat for the other arm.

2. Use pinking shears and cut at the line. Turn the jacket and arms inside out.

3. Fold the scarf lengthwise and cut it up the center so you have two strips of equal length.

4. Take one strip and, with the right sides of the fabric facing in, pin it around the raw edge of the sleeve. You will have to gather the scarf fabric as you pin, to create a flouncy effect. Sew in place, and then sew a second row. Repeat for the other sleeve.

5. Cut the bottom off the coat with the pinking shears to your desired length. Right below your waist is perfect, or even a bit lower, if you prefer. Pin the raw edges of the jacket and the scarf together, again—gathering the scarf as you pin. Sew in place, and then sew again.

6. Pin and sew rickrack around the collar, down the front, and anywhere else you want.

TIPS:

• Replace the buttons on your jacket with ones that match your scarf.

• If you can find only smaller scarves, buy several so you'll have enough.

• For a layered, ruffled look, add a second, longer row of the scarf behind the first one.

TENDING TO WOUNDS

In a perfect world, there would be no injuries in the creative arts. But honestly, in any kind of craft genre, if you don't pay attention and stay focused, you can get hurt. I accidentally nipped my finger under my fancy high-tech Janome Memory Craft 11000 while working on a project for this book. One morning I let myself get too confident—and in the next second I stood up and screamed. That needle had punctured my nail like a sunflower seed. This could have been avoided.

HERE IS THE CRAFTY CHICA CHECKLIST FOR PAIN-FREE STITCHING:

1. Always keep your fingers away from the guide. Before you stitch, look where they are positioned and move them away, if needed.

2. Don't get distracted by phone calls, the TV, or company. Sewing is not something that you want to multitask at.

3. Don't sit too long at your machine. Get up every forty minutes or so and walk around. Stretch your arms and back.

4. Make sure you have good posture. Sit up straight, make sure your table height is not awkward, and put a cushion on your chair.

5. When in doubt, use thimbles. They make them for all your fingers, and you can find them at the craft store. I use a meta-thimble when I'm sewing buttons on thick fabric or through pillows.

6. If you do happen to poke yourself with the needle, pour hydrogen peroxide on it and wrap it in a bandage. If your wound is serious, consult a doctor. But I know that will not happen, because you read these tips!

Revamped Mexicana
FLOWER BLOUSE

Flower blouses from Mexico are *muy fancy*. Made of light breezy cotton, they sport an explosion of colorful, embroidered flowers, vines, and leaves all across the top. The only problem? They all look the same after a while. But with just a bit of tweaking, you can update yours to a modern look without losing the classic style. And to that, let's say "*¡Viva!*" Note: You can find these blouses at Mexican import shops, or on eBay by searching under "Mexican peasant blouse."

SKILL LEVEL Intermediate

MATERIALS

1 Mexican flower blouse

1 black 50 percent polyester/50 percent cotton women's top

Straight pins

Pinking shears

1½ yd (137cm) of red trim

HOW TO MAKE IT

1. Turn the Mexican peasant blouse inside out, and, using the pinking shears, cut off the bottom portion 5" (12.5cm) down from the embroidered bustline (Diagram 1). Double-check your measurements before you cut!

2. Turn the black top inside out and cut it 12" (30.5cm) from the bottom hem (Diagram 2).

3. With the right side of the fabrics facing in, pin the raw edges of the two blouses together. **Important note:** The white blouse is made a bit puffy at the bottom, so you will have to lightly gather the fabric as you pin. This will give it a uniform look and distribute the extra fabric evenly. If you sew without gathering it a little bit, you will end up with big clump on one side!

4. Once it is pinned and looks perfect and even, sew it. Sew another row just above that (Diagram 3). Trim away excess fabric with pinking shears.

5. Pin the trim along the outside seam, from under the arm to the bottom of the hem. Sew it in place.

TIPS:

There are many ways to revamp this blouse:

• You can leave it as is, and embroider your own designs on the bottom portion of it.

• Cut the sleeves off, and hem the edges to make a tank.

• Sew various ribbons along the bottom.

1.

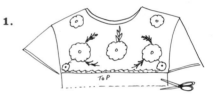

Black
Bottom

2.

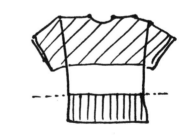

3.

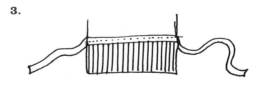

Turn right side out and sew ribbon on to front.

~ *Crafty Superstar* ~
JACKET

Whether you're a part-time crafter or a die-hard addict, chances are you have a nickname for your mad skills. If not, it's time to come up with one—pronto! Once you do, celebrate your witty title by making a crafty superstar jacket! Wear it to art shows, conventions, crafty shopping excursions, or even when you're making dinner. I made my jacket the night before a very important meeting. I was so nervous and had energy to burn, so I unleashed all that energy on an unsuspecting jacket via buttons, crystals, and glitter. Every time I wear it, I feel empowered. Especially when people stop me to comment on it.

SKILL LEVEL Easy to Intermediate to Difficult (your choice!)	Large foam letter stamps	Permanent spray-on fabric glitter
	Fabric paint	Assorted iron-on patches
MATERIALS	Fabric paintbrush	8–10 larger decorative buttons
1 jeans jacket	Permanent fabric adhesive	150 small buttons
1 cloth measuring tape	Glass crystals (about 300 3mm crystals, or 100 5–7mm crystals)	15–20 charms
Sewing needle		Embroidery thread and hoop
½ yd (45.5cm) jeweled trim	Heart stencil	

~ HOW TO MAKE IT ~

1. Start with the back of the jacket. Cut and sew the measuring tape up the sides. Hand-stitch the jeweled trim (Diagram 1).

2. Pick up a letter stamp with the first letter of your name and coat it with the fabric paint. Press it onto the fabric at the top of the jacket (Diagram 2). Repeat to spell out your name. Let dry. One by one, paint over each letter with the adhesive and add a crystal. Let dry.

3. Apply the stencil to the middle area of the jacket and add paint color (Diagram 3). Remove the stencil, paint the area with adhesive, and sprinkle on glitter. Let dry.

4. Iron on the patches.

5. Hand-sew the larger buttons, fill in with the smaller buttons, and then add the charms.

6. Attach the embroidery hoop and use the embroidery thread and needle to add stars or other accents.

7. Decorate the front of the jacket in the same fashion.

8. Spray on the glitter!

TIPS:

- If you don't want to use crystals for your name, you can paint over the letters with brush-on glitter varnish.

- After you apply your name, feel free to wear your jacket out and about. Work on it in stages.

- If your jacket comes out over-the-top wild, enter it in an art exhibit.

- If you belong to a craft group, have all the members make their own jackets and then wear them out together to a craft show or event.

- Sew up a fabric collage and use fusible webbing to iron it onto the back of the jacket.

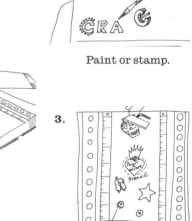

2.

Paint or stamp.

1.

3.

DIARY

~ of a ~

CRAFTY CHICA

FLASH ALERT! WHY EVERYONE NEEDS AN EMERGENCY SEWING KIT

Back in the day, I worked as an appeals clerk at Phoenix Municipal Court. My whole world revolved around scoring vintage dress clothes that I'd show off at my so-called prestigious office gig.

One morning I slipped past my boss, late as always, decked out in a '50s-era skin-hugging emerald suit. The extra fine sharkskin fabric had zero give, and with the skirt tight enough to cut off my circulation if I sat too long, I knew it would be a long day.

In my tiny office, I plopped down in the chair behind my desk, ready for the day's angry defendants to line up and file their appeal paperwork. And then—I heard it.

Rrrrrip!

My skirt's back center slit popped apart, along with part of the hem. After already being tardy, there was no way I could ask to go home. So I did the next best thing that any crafty working girl would do: I whipped out the Swingline stapler. I pulled down the shade on the Plexiglas service window, locked my door, took off my skirt, and performed press-n-punch surgery on the skirt's gashes.

Later, about five minutes before lunchtime, two hunky jocks rang the bell at the service window. I explained the appeal process, and one of them decided to proceed. I turned, walked to the front of my desk, bent over, and sifted through my files for the proper paperwork.

I returned to the window, and noticed both men grinning. Creepy grins that made the hairs stand up on the back of my neck. I handed the paperwork to the first guy and the other one cut in . . .

"Hey—I'd like to file an appeal too," he said, folding his arms over his chest and winking at his friend. "I want the same paperwork you got for him. Over there, from your desk."

"Weirdos," I thought. I politely turned around and walked to my desk again. When I came back to the window, they were both laughing. The first guy asked for another set. I knew something was up, but had no clue what it could be.

"Kathy, sit down—I'll take care of them," said a booming voice from across the office. It was my friend (and future husband) Patrick, who had arrived to take me to lunch. He signaled for me to have a seat, and then he gave the musclemen a homeboy glare of disgust as he approached the window.

I wondered why Patrick had such a rude attitude toward these men, since he had only walked in a second earlier. As soon as I sat down, I knew.

I felt the icy sting from my metal chair against the top of my back thigh.

I whisper-gasped in horror! My fancy hem job? Busted! Not only that, the staples had snagged on my pantyhose just above my bootie. No wonder those dudes wanted more paperwork. Every time I turned around and bent over, they saw all the junk in my trunk.

Crafty Chica Lesson Learned: Always carry a mini-sewing kit. Now reread that last sentence. Live it. Do it. Because you just never know when you—or someone else—will need an old school needle and thread. Keep one in your purse, your suitcase, and your office desk drawer. You can find small kits at the fabric store, or just make your own. Find a container like a small mint tin or lipstick case. Place inside your tin a couple needles, black and white thread, and if you can find some, a teeny set of scissors.

Chop Top
FROCK

Remember our father's dress shirts? Perfectly pressed, streamlined, and ready for power lunches. We chicas can use a bit of that corporate energy in our artsy lives. Here's a plan that uses a men's dress shirt as the base for a summer-friendly frock. Replace the buttons, chop the top, add a girlie-girl waistline, and you're ready to rock and roll.

SKILL LEVEL Advanced

MATERIALS

I men's dress shirt, blue (choose one that fits you a bit loosely)

Measuring tape

I package of ¼" (6mm) wide elastic

Straight pins

Red buttons

Fabric paint

Liner brush

Permanent fabric adhesive

Red fabric-friendly glitter

Red twill tape, ½" x 56" (13mm x 142cm)

Chopstick

Tape

HOW TO MAKE IT

1. Lay the shirt on a table in front of you. Measure 5" (12.5cm) above the chest pocket, and cut off the top of the shirt.

2. Sew a rolled hem (see page 35) to hide the raw edge on both sides of the top of the shirt. Now fold both sides over 1½" (3.8cm) and sew a straight stitch across. This will be the casing, or "tunnel," to hold the drawstring straps.

3. Turn the shirt inside out. Measure your rib cage and deduct 2" (5cm). Pull the elastic taut and cut a piece this size.

4. Pull the elastic tight and pin it all around the shirt, about ½" (13mm) under the pocket. Zigzag for ½" (13mm), and then switch to straight stitch. Zigzag when you reach the other end as well.

5. Remove the buttons from the shirt, and sew on the red ones.

6. Use fabric paint to add a design over the right chest area. Add fabric adhesive over the paint and then sprinkle on the glitter. Let dry.

7. Double up the twill tape and tape it to the end of a chopstick. Feed it through the casing at the top of the shirt, through the front, and then through the back. Two ends will come out on one side. Tie them in a bow. Scrunch the top of the shirt inward so your sexy shoulders will show!

TIPS:

- For more of a contrast, use the top of one shirt and the bottom of another.
- Embroider designs on your shirt.
- Wear a wide belt around your waist to accentuate it even more.
- Buy blank buttons and decorate them with glossy paint designs.

Stitch in Time

I have very bad karma when it comes to sewing. My grandmother used to have an old-fashioned Victorian machine that she used faithfully. When I was a little boy, I remember playing with it like a toy. I'd spin the hand wheel, and stomp on the foot pedal over and over until all her thread became one gigantic tangled mess. After all these years, I still feel guilty.

—PATRICK MURILLO, Phoenix, AZ

Kamikaze Fabric
SCRAP BELT

Belts are one of the best ways to transform a look. The bigger, chunkier, flashier, the better! And who knew you had all the supplies hanging around your room, maybe even in your trash bin. Collect all those little fabric scraps and unite them in the name of fashion!

SKILL LEVEL Intermediate

MATERIALS

A medium-sized pile of fabric scraps, each piece measuring approximately 2" (5cm)

Extra-firm interfacing, 2½" (6.5cm) x your waist measurement, plus 5" (12.5cm)

Straight pins

Grommet, and grommet tool

Belt buckle

Heavyweight thread

Sewing needle

HOW TO MAKE IT

(DIAGRAMS ON PAGE 90)

1. Arrange your scraps to form a long rectangle that measures 3" (7.5cm) x your waist measurement, plus 5" (12.5cm). Begin sewing the scraps together. Repeat until you have two long pieces (Diagram I).

2. Sandwich the interfacing between the two pieces of fabric. Sew down one side, with a ½" (13mm) seam allowance. Repeat on the other sides.

3. Trim excess fabric from the edges. Use the zigzag stitch to seam all four sides of the belt.

4. Put the belt around your waist and mark where you want the holes for the buckle to go.

5. Follow the manufacturer's directions for the grommet tool (Diagram 2).

6. Attach the buckle, and use heavyweight thread to hand-stitch it to the other end of the belt (Diagram 3).

TIPS:

- If you want your belt to have more wiggle room, add 6–7" (15–18cm) to the measurement instead of 5" (12.5cm).

- For a more polished look, turn in the edges on step 2 and sew.

- If you don't have a grommet tool or grommets, use an awl or a dremel to punch through the belt to make your holes. However, the grommets look nice and will make your belt last longer.

- Make a buckle to match! Buy a blank buckle and use your scraps to make a collage on the front. Glue on crystals for extra sparkle.

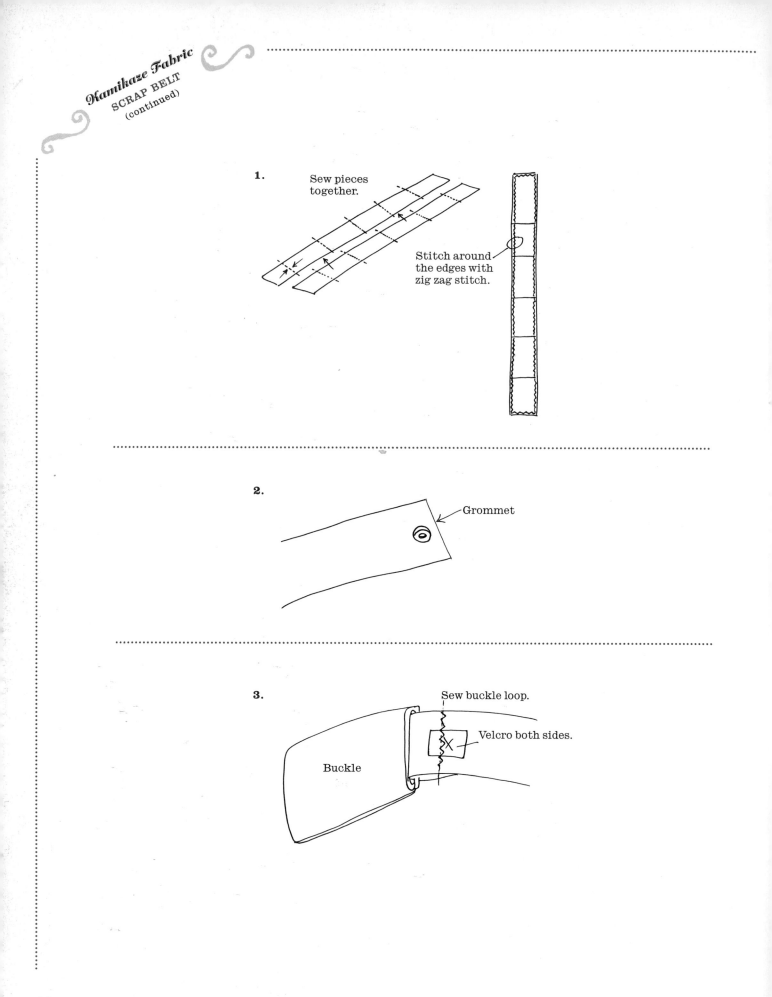

1.

Sew pieces
together.

Stitch around
the edges with
zig zag stitch.

2.

Grommet

3.

Sew buckle loop.

Velcro both sides.

Buckle

Black and White
RIBBON-TRIMMED PENCIL SKIRT

I've always said that I'm a fabric junkie. Well, I must admit that ribbon served as my gateway drug. I have more spools than my kids have socks. One day after watching an *Oprah* episode about extreme hoarders, I decided to cure myself once and for all. I decided to sew all my ribbon onto all my craft projects! One of the outcomes of that little binge is a black skirt adorned with nine different trims. I also added in buttons and yarn for good measure. No pun intended.

SKILL LEVEL Easy

MATERIALS
(to Make 1 Size 6 Decorated Skirt)

1 pencil skirt

1 yd (91cm) each of the following trims: rickrack, fringe, lace, metallic, stitched, polka dotted, plain, diagonal-lined

Straight pins

1 yd (91cm) chunky, multistrand black and white yarn

48 small buttons

Sewing needle

HOW TO MAKE IT

1. Lay the trims on the skirt and arrange them to your liking.
2. Pin them in place, row by row, and sew along the top.
3. Gather the yarn in spots so it looks naturally placed, and slowly sew over it using the zigzag stitch.
4. Hand-sew the buttons in the peaks and valley of the rickrack. Snip away excess threads.

TIPS:

- You can choose all the same type of ribbon.
- For a simple but textured look, use all black ribbons.
- If you feel daring and dramatic, add ribbons all the way up the skirt!
- Keep in mind: The larger the skirt, the more ribbon you'll need.

Pin & sew trim to your liking.

Sew yarn using zig zag stitch.

Hand sew buttons.

Work from bottom up.

Stitch in Time

Make sure you pin. It doesn't matter how great a sewer you think you are, fabric has a mind of its own! Also, press as you go, wow does that make a difference!

—MARK MONTANO,
celebrity designer, storeowner, author,
TV personality, www.markmontano.com

Summer SCARF DRESS

In every crafter's supply stash, there are usually a few one-of-a-kind items that are just too sweet to be cut or altered. Like vintage scarves! Sure you can sew a collection of them together to make a duvet cover, or maybe just two for a silky toss pillow, but how about a dress? This design makes use of the scarves' details in a fun, flowy fashion, perfect for a trip to the beach! Any 36" (91cm) scarves can be used, but if you want vintage ones, visit a local antique store or eBay.

SKILL LEVEL Easy

MATERIALS

3 scarves of your choice, 36" x 36" (91cm x 91cm)

Straight pins

Lightweight sewing machine needle

1 tube top

3 yd (2.75m) ribbon

HOW TO MAKE IT

(DIAGRAMS ON PAGE 96)

1. Pin the three scarves together in a row (Diagram 1). If they have a picture, make sure to sew them all in the same direction.

2. Turn the tube top inside out and, starting at the front of the tube top, just below the bustline, pin the top of the scarf to the dress. Continue to pin, but make sure to pinch and gather the fabric about $\frac{1}{8}$" (3mm) every inch (2.5cm) or so (Diagram 2). This will give the scarves a nice fluid look.

3. Once it is pinned on, carefully sew it in place, removing the pins as you go (Diagram 3).

4. Pin the ribbon around the seam you just sewed (Diagram 4). Stitch it in place so the two ends hang in the front of the dress. Tie them in a small bow.

TIPS:

- If you want the scarves to be thicker, pin and sew a piece of sheer lining onto them before you pin them on the dress.
- If you only have two scarves, do not gather the scarf piece at the top as much.
- To remove wrinkles, steam your dress.

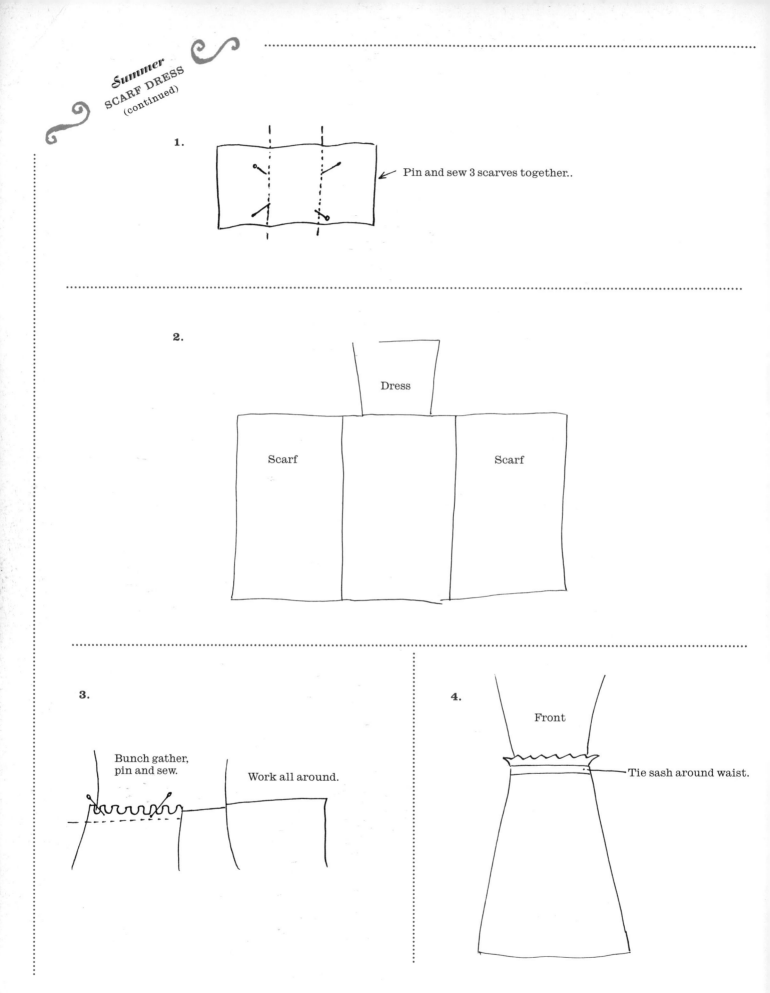

1. Pin and sew 3 scarves together..

2. Dress

Scarf   Scarf

3. Bunch gather, pin and sew.

Work all around.

4. Front

Tie sash around waist.

3

EMBRACE YOUR SPACE

La casa FELIZ.

La maison heureuse.

The happy home!

Your living space is the most important setting in your life. It doesn't matter if it's as big as a Hollywood mansion or as small as a matchbox—it's your personal digs. You need to feel cozy and comfy enough to stretch, relax, sing, dance, sing, yell, sleep, and read at any given moment. Shopping for furniture and accessories is only the beginning. The next step is to work your creative magic with a little help from your sewing machine. These ideas are sure to point you in the right direction. By now you know I'm a sucker for bright, crazy color and patterns. It's OK if you have more subdued taste—I'm not offended! Simply take the technique or application and alter it so that you will love it and be proud to have it in your house. That's why we make things in the first place, right?

Rough and Ruffled PLACE MATS

The best meals are the ones that burst with a variety of flavors, textures, colors, and shapes. With a combination platter like that, you'll need a placemat to match. This design is thick with ruffles, yet is sturdy enough for a ten-course meal. It takes the elegant, fluffy concept of chenille (fringed fabric) and combines it with different materials like jersey, cotton, ribbon and fleece. The best part? It has so many grooves and crevices, it will hide any fallen crumbs!

SKILL LEVEL Easy

MATERIALS

1 cloth placemat, black

12 pieces of red jersey fabric, 3" x 3" (7.5cm x 7.5cm)

4 pieces of fuchsia leece fabric, 9" x 3" (23cm x 7.5cm)

4 pieces of printed cotton fabric, 6½" x 3" (16.5cm x 7.5cm)

16 pieces of white jersey fabric, 2" x 3" (5cm x 7.5cm)

1 piece of teal jersey fabric, 6" x 6" (15cm x 15cm)

4 pieces of fabric, 9" x 3" (23cm x 7.5cm)

8 pieces of fabric, maroon woven jersey, 3" x 3" (7.5cm x 7.5cm)

3 types of ribbon that are contrasting in color

Assorted colors of threads

1 yd of large pompom fringe, black

HOW TO MAKE IT:

(DIAGRAMS ON PAGE 102)

1. Sort all of the pieces in stacks of four, keeping like fabrics together (Diagram 1).

2. Take one piece of each, and lay them on the placemat according to the picture shown. If you have overage, trim to fit, keeping in mind that jersey fabric will stretch as you sew.

3. Remove the pieces. Start at the bottom left, take the stack of printed cotton fabric and lay it on the placemat. Sew five horizontal lines, each one ½" (2.5cm) apart from the other (Diagram 2).

4. Now pick up four pieces of the red jersey fabric, lay down flush left, and sew lines in the same fashion.

5. Take the second set of four, and sew those in place with vertical lines.

6. Continue sewing down the remaining stacks of fabric. Make sure to sew each portion in a different direction, because this is what will give your placemat an interesting look.

7. Once they are all sewed down, take your scissors and snip through the channels between the rows of stitches (Diagram 3).

8. Machine wash and tumble-dry the placemat, for ultimate ruffles (Diagram 4)!

9. Cut and sew swatches of ribbon between each of the fabrics.

10. Sew on the pompom fringe (Diagram 5).

TIPS:

- Use old T-shirts, or other unwanted clothing items.
- Look for fabric that has interesting accents, like metallic foils, embroidery, or patterns.
- Use contrasting thread to sew over your ribbon.
- Incorporate patches or fabric images.
- Embroider on top of the ruffles for more detail.
- Frame your placemats if you don't want to use them.
- Use this concept on anything from table runners and pillows to purses and dresses.

Stitch in Time

My grandmother could sew anything and make it look amazing. It was her one guilty pleasure and because of that, I never asked her to teach me how to sew. I deeply regret that now as I'm hopelessly spastic around a sewing machine, yet I persevere in spite of myself. One of these days, I'm going to take the time to master sewing, but until then it's kamikaze stitching for this Impatient Seamstress!

—MARGOT POTTER, Pennsylvania, author, designer, TV personality www.margotpotter.com

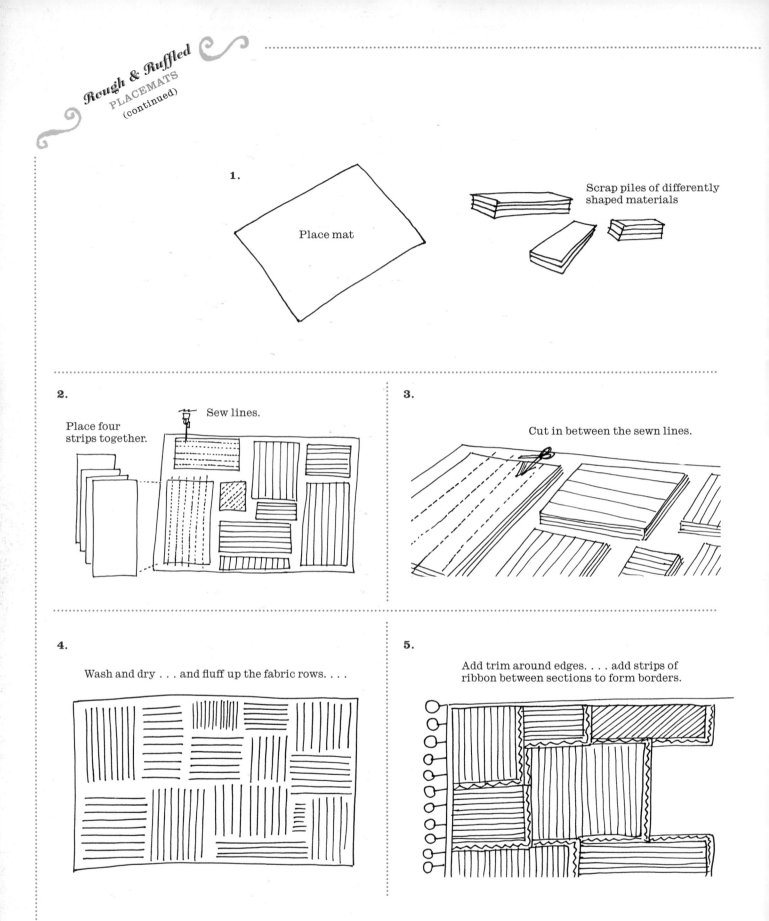

1.

Place mat

Scrap piles of differently shaped materials

2.

Place four strips together.

Sew lines.

3.

Cut in between the sewn lines.

4.

Wash and dry . . . and fluff up the fabric rows. . . .

5.

Add trim around edges. . . . add strips of ribbon between sections to form borders.

～ *Lush Life* ～
LOUNGE PILLOWS

Napkins are useful for more than just table dressing or wiping cake frosting from your lips. They also make perfect pillows. Don't they look like they came from a high-end department store? No one will ever guess that they were made in a matter of minutes at your sewing table!

SKILL LEVEL Easy

MATERIALS

2 black and white patterned napkins, 20" x 20" (51cm x 51cm)

Straight pins

1 bag of Fiberfil stuffing, 20 oz (567g)

2 large black buttons

1 large tapestry needle

Embroidery thread

～ HOW TO MAKE IT ～

1. Line up the napkins, right side out. Pin three sides, and halfway up the fourth. Make sure the hems are lined up evenly.

2. Sew, removing the pins as you go.

3. In the remaining opening, fill the pillow with the Fiberfil, stuffing it into the corners and filling the pillow so it is firm but still has some give.

4. Pin and sew the opening closed. Pat the pillow to make the stuffing look balanced.

5. Thread the tapestry needle with embroidery thread and sew on the button through the center of the pillow. That will be challenge because of all the stuffing, but keep working to poke the needle through the center of the other side. Tip: Watch your fingers as you are poking the needle through! Once you get the needle through the center of the other side, stitch on the next button, and then poke the needle back through to the first side. Repeat twice on each side to make sure that the buttons are sewn on securely.

TIPS:

- Look for napkins that look like they are made from expensive fabrics.
- You can make rectangular pillows by using placemats.
- Add trim or iron-on accents.
- Sew several napkins together to make a large floor pillow or pet bed.
- Make small Pillow Stix by using the napkins and following the directions on page 124.

Stitch in Time

"When I was in 8th grade, my mom taught me how to embroider. I went with it, and became really good. That same year, there was this girl I fell in love with, so I embroidered her a beautiful shirt. It took me forever—it had a sunset and all these detailed flowers. I was so proud of it. Soon after I gave it to her, I went to her house, and what did I see? Her dog sleeping on top of my creation! I never embroidered again."

—JOHN SAMORA, Phoenix, AZ

~ Second Chance ~
CURTAIN CALL

Room makeovers are more affordable than you think. Instead of ditching all your goods, give them a second chance instead. Take your drapes, for instance. All that fabric! You can follow in the footsteps of Scarlett O'Hara and have your maid make you a dress—or you can take matters into your own hands and recycle them. The secret is slicing the panels into skinny strips, and then inserting a contrasting pattern. Add some tabs at the top and you have a new look for your room!

SKILL LEVEL Easy

MATERIALS

1 panel solid-color curtains, 82" x 84" (208cm x 213cm)

2 yd (1.8m) patterned fabric that matches the solid-color curtains

Straight pins

~ HOW TO MAKE IT: ~

1. Cut the solid-color curtains into eight strips that measure 72" x 5" (183cm x 12.5cm). Repeat for the patterned fabric.

2. Separate them into two groups of eight (four of each).

3. Start with the first set. Pin the strips together vertically, right sides in. Alternate between solid and patterned pieces. Sew, and remove pins as you go.

4. Sew a rolled hem (see page 35) all the way around your new curtain panel.

5. Repeat steps 3 and 4 for the second set.

HOW TO MAKE TOP TABS

To make your curtains even longer (which will make your ceiling look higher!), you'll want to make top tabs to sew to the top edge.

1. With the fabric from the leftover solid color drapes, cut 16 pieces that measure 3" x 6" (7.5cm x 15cm).

2. Take one piece, turn it inside out, and sew around three sides. Now turn each one right side out. Fold in the raw edges and sew. Repeat for the remaining tabs.

3. Fold one tab in half and pin one tab to the top of one of the strips. Working from left to right, repeat for the remaining pieces. Sew each one in place.

TIPS:

- To make heavier and thicker curtains, sew a lining to the back.
- For a more subdued look, choose solid color fabric, instead of a patterned one.
- For a more bohemian look, sew strips of ribbon down the seams and/or add fringe along the bottom or top.

Stitch in Time

I was about nine years old when the movie *E.T.* came out. I wanted an ET doll in the worst way. My parents refused ("Too expensive!" "Ugly!"). But my mother offered to help me make one. I learned a lot by seeing how my mother did the construction. She gave me a pillowcase, and knowing how much I loved to draw, suggested that I draw ET on the case. I watched as she cut out the shape, sandwiched it wrong sides together, and sewed it up, leaving a small opening. She then gave it to me for stuffing and closed the opening. I made about ten more ET dolls after that, and forever learned the simplest construction technique, which is still the only way I know how to sew!

—JENNY HART, Austin, Texas, artist, designer, author, www.sublimestitching.com

chica power

Post Card

place
stamp
here

~9~ *Frivolous Fabric* ~C~
POSTCARDS

Once you get in the groove of pinning and stitching, you'll want to sew everything in your path. Even the mail. Making your own postcards is fun, fast, and will let the recipients know you think oh-so-much of them. Not to mention that your local postman will smile at your cleverness. One batch will take about an hour and then you can decide which to mail and which to frame and hang as artwork!

SKILL LEVEL Easy

MATERIALS

Assorted pieces of fabric, 4" x 6" each (10cm x 15cm)

Straight pins

Pieces of heavy interfacing, 4" x 6" each (10cm x 15cm)

Assorted fabric images cut out from other pieces of fabric

Crafty Chica postcard template (page 133), printed and cut out from fabric paper

Assorted ribbons and trims

~9~ HOW TO MAKE IT ~C~

1. Start with one piece of 4" x 6" (10cm x 15cm) fabric. This will be for one postcard. Arrange other fabric images on it to make a mini-collage.

2. Pin and sew the pieces in place, using the zigzag stitch so the edges will not fray.

3. Sandwich a piece of the interfacing between the collage and the Crafty Chica postcard backing. Zigzag stitch all around the edges.

4. Cut any stray threads.

TIPS:

- Add a little bit of batting between your fabric pictures to give them a dimensional look.

- Print your own artwork on fabric paper and use that for your postcards.

- Make a set of six postcards, apply a stamp to each one, tie them up with a ribbon, and give them as a gift to friends or family who are going away on a trip (within the United States, of course).

- You can also use iron-on decals or appliqués!

Color-It-Yourself
LOVER PILLOWCASE

Fancy fabric is a luxury if you're short on cash. No worries. There are a multitude of money-saving alternatives if you're in the mood for pedal pressing. Making your own pillowcase is just one way. Light cotton fabric is always affordable (especially if you come across a store coupon!), and there are a zillion ways to decorate it so it looks cool and smart, too. This design steps into the world of juicy fabric markers. They can be mixed and used for shading, but what I like most is that they add serious levels of color without the trouble or mess of wet paint. And you know what? Go right ahead and splurge on that fancy fabric; after all, you'll only need ¼ yd (23cm) of it!

SKILL LEVEL Intermediate

MATERIALS

1 piece white cotton fabric, 27″ x 40″ (68.5cm x 101.5cm)

1 piece heart-themed fabric (not pictured in photo), 10″ x 40″ (25.5cm x 101.5cm)

Iron and pressing cloth

Templates from page 134

1 dissolving ink fabric marking pen

1 piece cardboard to slip inside while you color

Broad fabric markers (red, orange, purple)

HOW TO MAKE IT

1. Use your zigzag stitch to sew around all the raw edges of both the white cotton fabric and the heart fabric.

2. Fold the white cotton fabric in half so it measures 27″ x 20″ (70cm x 51cm). Press the crease.

3. Photocopy the heart, crown, and sash templates from pages 132 and 133. Cut them out and center the heart and crown onto the white cotton fabric, and trace the shapes with the fabric marking pen. Trace the sash pattern on top of the heart.

4. Use the zigzag stitch to outline the image.

5. Fold the heart fabric lengthwise and press along the crease so you have a piece of folded fabric that measures 5″ x 40″ (12.5cm x 101.5cm).

6. Open the white cotton fabric, and pin the bottom of the heart fabric ¼″ (6mm) underneath the long side of it. Sew it in place, removing pins as you go.

7. Turn the whole thing right side in, and sew around the three sides.

8. Turn it right side out. Sew a decorative stitch where the trim and the body of the pillowcase meet.

9. Insert the cardboard and color in the design.

TIPS:

- Come up with your own designs to sew as outlines on the pillowcase.
- Use store-bought letter stencils to spell out a name.
- Use markers in different colors to add more accents.
- Customize the size of your pillowcase by increasing or decreasing the measurements.

Stitch in Time

Here is the one bit of geometry I have learned. Pi multiplied by the diameter of a circle equals the circumference of that circle. The circumference is the distance around the perimeter of a circle. The diameter is the distance across the center of a circle. Pi is a constant number, 3.14, that represents the ratio of the diameter to the circumference. In other words, the circumference is going to be 3.14 times the diameter. Therefore, the next time you need to figure out how many inches or centimeters there are around your round pillow, circle skirt, or tablecloth just measure the distance across that circle and multiple that number by 3.14. *Voilà!* All is revealed.

—FREDDA PERKINS, McKinney, Texas, craft expert

~ Family Circle ~
PHOTO ALBUM

Creating fabric scrapbooks has been a long-time hobby of mine. But rectangles and squares become boring after a while. So I present to you a geeky twist on the traditional family "album"! Literally. One guess what's inside these pages—vinyl record albums! They give the book some substance and fit just right with the theme.

SKILL LEVEL Intermediate

MATERIALS

6 pieces of fabric cut in circles, 12" (30.5cm) in diameter

6 pieces fabric cut in circles, 14" (35.5cm) in diameter

Straight pins

Assorted family photos printed on fabric paper (with peel-off backing)

Assorted patches, fabric images, buttons

Embroidery needle and embroidery thread

3 unwanted vinyl record albums

3 pieces of batting cut in circles, 12" (30.5cm) in diameter

6 pieces trim for each page, 1 yd (91cm) each

3 large buttons

Permanent fabric adhesive

Fabric-friendly glitter, or fabric squeeze glitter

Sewing needle and thread

Assorted charms

~ HOW TO MAKE IT ~

1. Pin and sew the smaller pieces of circle fabric to the center of the larger ones, so you have six "pages."

2. Embellish each page by sewing on fabric photos, ironing on patches, embroidering, etc.

3. To make your first double-sided page, sandwich the album like this: fabric, batting, album, batting, fabric. Pin around the edges, and sew. Repeat the process for the other two album pages.

4. Line up the pages and know that you will be binding the book on the left side by sewing a 7" (18cm) seam. Mark this off on each page with a pin. Now sew the trim around the edges of each album page, but not where the 7" seam will be.

5. Sew the seam.

6. Thread the embroidery needle and sew a button on where the hole is in the record on every page.

7. Accent areas with fabric adhesive and glitter. Let dry. Hand-sew on charms.

TIPS:

- Use fabric paint and letter stamps to add names to your book.
- Use images from old T-shirts.
- Keep in mind that once you put the book together, you will not be able to sew anything else on it, but you can use hot glue to affix some last-minute additions.
- This a great project for musicians in your family, or a way to celebrate your family's favorite songs.
- Decorate a page for each family member.

DIARY
～ of a ～
CRAFTY CHICA

Some of the most exciting moments in my crafty career have come from TV appearances. The false eyelashes, the flashy sets, the director yelling, "Gimme the money shot, chica!"

Oh sure, from your end of the boob tube, everything looks fine. The finished project glimmers under the Hollywood lights, the instructions go as smooth as silk. Ha! If only you knew what went on behind the seams, errr, I mean scenes.

I've had a news anchor take a bite out of my crafty masterpiece (a chocolate tree) five seconds before airtime. I once hit another anchor on the head with a painted egg (on live TV). I even forgot how to crochet the night before I was to demo a simple iPod cozy on a national craft show. I'm proud to say that I managed to keep my cool during all those high-stress moments. However, one time I came *thisclose* to having an all-out anxiety attack.

I was set to travel to Burbank, California with my craft group, the Phoenix Fridas. We were all excited to film three episodes that focused on our sewing skills. For once, I wanted to be prepared. A week before, I made my project and step-outs. I then sketched out an outfit I would make for my appearance: a cute red jersey tee with a handmade appliqué on the front.

I went with my then-twelve-year-old daughter, Maya, to Target to buy the shirt. Maya wanted one, too. I bought my size 1X version, and her XS. We arrived home, my attention was diverted, the week passed—and the next thing I knew, it was departure day. I had exactly thirty minutes to construct my masterpiece.

"No worries," I thought. "I could make this in my sleep!" I whipped it together, and it looked even better than my sketch. I packed it in my suitcase, and off I went.

Fast forward to the Burbank Studio, fifteen minutes to taping. My fellow Fridas prepped and primped in our shared dressing room. I took care of everything at the hotel, so all I had to do was change into my red top. I waited until minutes before to make sure that I wouldn't spill anything on my precious creation.

"It's time, Fridas!" hollered the floor manager.

I asked all the Fridas to leave. I'm ultra-shy. I don't dare let anyone see me change my clothes, even my best friends. Plus-size chicas are modest like that. They left the room, and I excitedly popped up off my chair. I retrieved my sacred T-shirt and slipped off my icky black blouse.

I lifted the red shirt before my face —and gulped.

Size 1X it was not. In the heat of racing against the clock, I realized that I had accidentally embellished Maya's XS shirt. I got them mixed up—they were both red!

My heart raced. My left eyeball throbbed. I poked my head out the door, and yelled for my friend. "Anita! Come here, quick, I need help! Please! It's an emergency!"

In that moment I thought perhaps by some weird chance, the shirt might fit. So I forced it over my head. Bad move. It scraped over my face like a stocking, and stopped at my neck.

I began to choke. Wearing only a Lane Bryant gladiator-looking bra and a black skirt. With a twelve-year-old's tiny T-shirt sucking the life out of me.

In between my frantic gasps for air and my hands clawing at my face, I saw through the jersey knit that not only had Anita arrived—she also brought the other Fridas: Keri and Carmen. My eyes darted to the left and I made out another figure—Oh God. The wardrobe lady, Jane. So much for modesty.

Anita helped me peel off the offending garment. Jane attempted to comfort me by flicking her wrist at me, and saying: "Don't worry kid, this happens all the time." Keri and Carmen politely left the room.

I had no other shirt to wear, and the director needed us on the set. Jane and Anita promised to make it work. Sure enough, Anita pulled out a pair of scissors and cut the shirt all the way up the back, and then made a long slit up each side. We then cut off the collar with pinking shears in a square design and removed the sleeves.

"OK, now try it," Anita said.

I closed my eyes, recited a round of power prayers, and put it over my head. It worked! Basically, my genius design had been pared down to flap in front of my torso. At least the cute appliqué stayed put.

Jane grabbed a light black rayon jacket that I had brought, and put it on me. "Don't lift your arms! Don't even move!" she warned. Anita gave me a hug and we raced out of the room to film our segment. I did my best robot impersonation that day for fear that my little secret would be exposed.

These days, our craft group laughs at the memory. Especially Anita. I still have that shirt. And yes. I do plan to sew it to another shirt someday. Size 1X, of course!

Crafty Chica Lesson Learned: Do your best to plan ahead. Especially if you are making an outfit to wear for a big event—like a national TV show. When you finish it, try it on to make sure it fits right. And I can't stress enough that crafty friends are wonderful to have in your life. Whether you're into sewing, beading, writing, anything—look for other people with like interests. They'll always have your back!

Bohemian
BED COVER

Have you ever come across something like a wall hanging you love but don't know what to do with? My advice is to buy it anyway. I'm really into anything that has a world culture feel or look to it, and when I came across this inexpensive Indian covering/tablecloth, I knew it was destiny. I bought two and made them into one lightweight bed cover that is not only snuggle-friendly, but chic, too. The best part about this project is that it is like making a quilt without all the effort!

SKILL LEVEL Easy

MATERIALS

2 wall coverings, 72" x 60"
(183cm x 152.5cm)

I piece of batting, 71" x 59"
(180cm x 150cm)

Metallic trim, fringe or rickrack, 7½ yd
(7m) (optional)

Embroidery needle and thread

Assorted iron-on crystals

HOW TO MAKE IT

(DIAGRAMS ON PAGE 120)

1. Lay one of the coverings face down on the floor. (Make sure your floor is clean!), and then lay the batting on top of that. Now add the second covering face up on top of that (Diagram 1).

2. Pin around the border 3" (7.5cm) from the edge. Sew.

3. Sew around the edge.

4. Pin and sew on the rickrack around the edge (Diagram 2).

5. In order to keep the batting secure, thread the embroidery needle and sew little starbursts randomly throughout the center (Diagram 3).

6. Iron on the crystals.

TIPS:

- For a thicker feel, double or even triple the batting.
- Use binding tape around the edges for a more polished look.
- Give it a silky feel by using a satiny fabric on the back—but you'll have to sew a rolled hem around the edges.
- If you don't have a second wall covering, just use a sheet for the back and cut it to size.

Two sides with batting in between . . .

1.

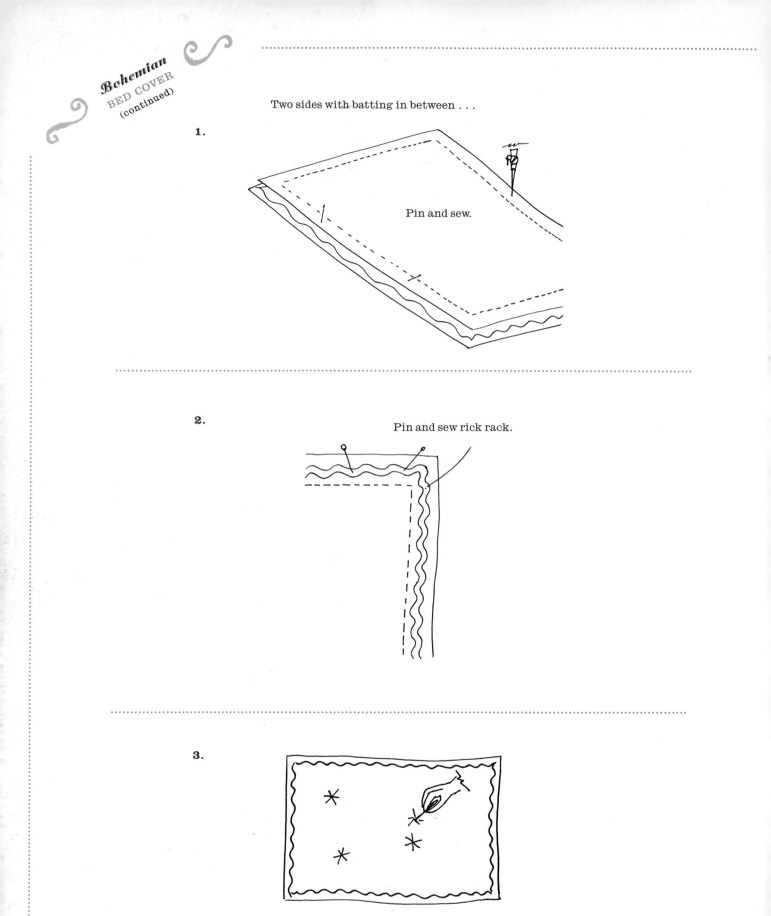

Pin and sew.

2.

Pin and sew rick rack.

3.

Hand sew star bursts randomly
to secure batting.

Iron on crystals.

~ *Canvas Kaleidoscope* ~
FLOOR CLOTH

Painted floor cloths have been around longer than Legos. They are usually decorated in the same formulaic fashion: Rectangles, circles, squares, maybe an oval or an octagon here or there. I say we pump our fists above our heads and start a floor cloth revolution! Are you with me? Let's chant together: "Cut it up! Cut it up!" Let me explain. Slice and dice pieces of primed canvas, paint them, and sew them together to make a mosaic/ kaleidoscope-looking design.

SKILL LEVEL Easy to Intermediate

MATERIALS

1 pad primed canvas sheets, 12" x 16" (30.5cm x 40.5cm) in size

Petal template on page 135

Acrylic paints in assorted colors

Paintbrush

Letter or chunky foam stamps

Metallic paint pen

Fabric-friendly glitter

Permanent fabric adhesive

Liner brush

Brush or spray-on polyurethane varnish

Nonslip rug guards

~ HOW TO MAKE IT ~

1. Make a copy of the petal pattern and use it to cut out 13 petals from the canvas sheets.

2. Basecoat each petal in your desired colors. Let each one dry, and add more painted accents, freehand or with foam stamps. Highlight with the metallic paint pen.

3. Add glitter by using the liner brush to apply fabric adhesive. Sprinkle on the glitter and tap away the excess. Let dry.

4. Seam all the petal edges by sewing with a tight zigzag stitch.

5. Arrange the pieces in a flower pattern, and, using the zigzag stitch, sew them together one petal at a time.

6. Apply three coats of brush-on or spray-on high gloss polyurethane varnish, and let it dry between each coat. Add nonslip rug guards on the bottom.

TIPS:

• Use the paint pen to write your favorite phrases.

• Get creative and find all kinds of other shapes to make a floor cloth.

• If you want to stick with a rectangular or circular shape, you can. Just sew the separate painted pieces together to fit the size.

MAKE YOUR OWN CAR MATS
Use your existing car mat as a template.

Pillow STIX

Pillows are one of best and easiest sewing projects for beginners. The lines are clean and the edges always crisp. If you've mastered this but aren't quite ready to dive into designing drapes or dresses, here's a project that will exercise your curves. These pillow stix are ultra-mod and super-flirty, and they make for impressive pillow-fighting artillery. For the best effect, make several of these in color-coordinated fabrics. Use them on your couch, bed, patio—anywhere!

SKILL LEVEL Easy

MATERIALS

1 piece of fabric 16" x 24" (40.5 x 61cm)

Straight pins

2 circles of fabric, 5½" (14cm) in diameter

Fiberfil, 20 oz (567g)

HOW TO MAKE IT

1. Take the large piece of fabric, fold it in half lengthwise, and with the right side in, sew the raw edges together lengthwise. Sew another row. You will have a long sleeve.

2. Take one of the circles and attach it to one end of the sleeve with pins, making sure to fold the raw ends in. Once it is all pinned, sew it in place.

3. Stuff the sleeve with the Fiberfil, packing it tight all the way to the top.

4. Repeat step 2 to close off the pillow.

TIPS:

- Add fringe or trim around the circles.
- Extend the measurements to make even longer pillows.
- Make some for a child's room. Ask your child to paint some cotton fabric and use that for the pillows.

USE SEWING TO REFRESH YOUR HOME DECOR

One machine, so many ideas. You have the power to add new accents to your living room, patio, bedroom—any room—just by using your skills. Here are some easy ideas of other items to make for your *casa azucar*.

- Sew place mats together to make floor mats, throw rugs, or table runners.
- Fold a fabric place mat lengthwise and sew vertical lines in it. Sew a long ribbon to the end so you can roll it up and to tie it off. Now you have a case for makeup brushes, art brushes, markers, etc. You can also fold it widthwise to make a holder for small travel items.
- Pretty cloth place mats also make great mini-pillows or clutch purses.
- Use leftover fabric and batting to make potholders, or even—yes! Place mats!
- Sew small sachets to keep in your closet or dresser.
- For easy wall art, sew stripes together of color-coordinated fabric and staple them around a canvas. Make a set of three and hang them.
- Use tablecloths to make curtains, giant floor pillows, or a duvet cover.
- Measure the circumference of a big roomy lampshade. Cut small squares of fabric, and sew them up in metallic thread in a piece to fit your lampshade. Wrap the piece around a lampshade (attach it with spray adhesive).
- Sew pretty fringe or lace on sheer fabric and use it to drape across your ceilings or at the top of your window coverings.
- Use the directions for the oilcloth tote on page 46 to make a cover for your coffee maker, sewing machine, or computer monitor. (You'll have to change the measurements.)
- Make easy slipcovers to go over the backs of your chairs.

~ Family Fragment ~
FABRIC COLLAGE

We should always be proud of our families and showcase their pictures in our homes. It means even more when you can score vintage photos of your grandparents when they were kids. Ask to borrow photos from your family members so you can scan them into your computer and use them to make something like this art collage. That's exactly what I did with the images of my husband's family.

SKILL LEVEL Easy

MATERIALS

9 fabric images, approximately 2½" (6.5cm) —edges cut with pinking shears.

9 pieces scrap fabric in each of the following sizes:

3" x 4½" (7.5 x 11.5cm): Fabric A

5" x 4½" (12.5cm x 11.5cm): Fabric B

1 piece contrasting fabric, 18" x 15" (45.5cm x 38cm)

1 piece heavyweight fabric, 22" x 18" (56cm x 45.5cm)

1 piece of contrasting fabric, 18" x 15" (45.5 x 38 cm)

Sequin trim, 20" (51cm)

Metallic trim, 12" x 15" (30.5cm x 38cm)

Cream lace, 22" (56cm)

Pompom fringe, 22" (56cm)

1 dowel, ½" x 24" (13mm x 61cm)

~ HOW TO MAKE IT ~

1. Match up one photo with one of the fabric A pieces, pin it, and sew it on top. Repeat with the others.

2. Sew each of these pieces to each of the fabric B pieces, until you have nine pieces.

3. Pin and then sew them in three rows of three. Sew the three rows together so you have one large panel with nine photos.

4. Take the 18" x 15" (45.5cm x 38cm) piece of fabric and cut the edges to look curvy. Pin it in the center of the 22" x 28" piece of fabric. Sew it in place.

5. Sew the picture panel in the center of that.

6. Sew the metallic trim around the border of the picture panel. Add any other decorative stitching that you'd like.

7. Sew the lace to the bottom, and then sew the pompom fringe.

8. Seam all the raw edges by using the zigzag function.

9. At the top of the collage, fold the top edge to the back and sew it in place to make the casing for the dowel. Sew a second row. Insert the dowel and hang it.

TIPS:

- If you don't have vintage photos, but still want the look, print your photos out in black and white or sepia tone.

- This is a great way to make use of scrap fabric and trims.

- You can also add in vintage handwritten letters by printing them onto fabric paper.

Stitch in Time

In my eighth-grade home ec class, it was the night before our final project of the semester was due and, like any normal thirteen-year-old, I procrastinated. I finally sat down and watched the *Johnny Carson Show*, thinking I could zip through my project. I looked at my pattern with bewilderment. It might as well have been a map of the New York subway system in Japanese. I was lost. Confused. Frustrated. At about 3 a.m. and one *Too Close for Comfort* episodes too many, I said, "Forget it!" I grabbed one of my mom's hand-sewing needles, and made one- and two-inch (2.5cm and 5cm), hand-sewn stitches around my shorts. I turned them in and miraculously got a C. But guess what? My cousin wore those shorts for nearly three years before those stitches gave out!"

—THERESA CANO, Phoenix AZ

TEMPLATES

LOVER

WEBSITES
TO BRING OUT YOUR INNER GLITTER

A DRESS A DAY: A celebration of women's clothing from the past, present, and future. www.dressaday.com.

BUST: For feminist, edgy chicas who like to craft and kick butt. www.bust.com.

CAMP SARK: Dedicated to helping men and women find their inner child. www.campsark.com

CRAFT GOSSIP BLOG NETWORK: a wealth of insider info for crafty chicas everywhere. www.craftgossip.com

CRAFTSTER.ORG: A huge community of clever crafters who post their ideas and pictures of completed projects. www.craftster.org

CRAFT STYLISH: Charming goodies, inspirations and ideas! www.craftstylish.com

CRAFTY CHICA: My website, which offers free craft projects, articles on crafting trends, creativity tips, and mucho mas! www.craftychica.com.

CRAFT ZINE: Hundreds of postings of projects and ideas by crafters from around the world. Craftzine.com.

DIVA TRIBE: A community and resource site for smart, courageous, and artistic women. www.divatribe.com.

GET CRAFTY: Making art out of everyday life from cooking and cleaning to crafting and clubbing. www.getcrafty.com.

PURSE STORIES: Entertaining site where women write and post stories about their favorite accessory of all time—purses! www.pursestories.com.

SEW GREEN: A blog about sewing the eco-good life, handmade style. sewgreen.blogspot.com.

SKIRT! MAGAZINE: A saucy site for sassy ladies who love to play, dream, shop, and work. www.skirtmag.com

SUPERNATURALE: A cyber-gathering place for creative, crafty, and clever women. www.supernaturale.com

THE SWITCHBOARDS: Directory and community site for arts and crafts business owners. www.theswitchboards.com.

THREADBANGER: Videos of clever ideas for altering clothing and more. Threadbanger.com.

WARDROBE REFASHION: One woman's pledge to make everything she wears—and motivate others to do the same. nikkishell.typepad.com/ wardroberefashion.

WHIP UP: "Handcraft in a hectic world." Whipup.net.

SEWING MACHINE

~ COMPANIES ~

I used two machines for this book: Janome Memory Craft 11000 and a Singer 30-Stitch Function Sewing Machine 8280. Here's a list of all the sewing machine companies, just in case you always wanted to know!

BABY LOCK: babylock.com

BERNINA: berninausa.com
630-978-2500

BROTHER: brother.com

DREAM WORLD: dreamworld-inc.com
800-837-3261

ELNA: elna.com
905-821-0266 x 225

HUSQVARNA/VIKING:
husqvarnaviking.com/us/
800-358-0001

JANOME: janome.com

KENMORE: sears.com
800-549-4505

PFAFF: pfaffusa.com

SINGER: singerco.com
800-4-SINGER

WHITE: whitesewing.com
800-331-3164

CRAFT GROUPS

~ & ORGANIZATIONS ~

AMERICAN CRAFT COUNCIL:
craftcouncil.org.
212-274-0630

AMERICAN SEWING GUILD:
asg.org.
713-729-3000

CHURCH OF CRAFT:
www.churchofcraft.org

CRAFT AND HOBBY ASSOCIATION:
www.hobby.org
201-835-1211

HOME SEWING ASSOCIATION:
www.sewing.org
412-372-5950

MEET UP: sewing.meetup.com

ACKNOWLEDGMENTS

Thank you most to my Nana Cano up in heaven. She was a master seamstress, and I know she watched over my shoulder to make sure everything within these covers went smooth and shiny.

And if it were not for all the crafty people in the world, this book would not have been possible. I am so thankful for everyone who has visited my site, bought and read my books, used my craft products, watched my TV segments—you are the reason I keep sprinkling the glitter!

I owe all the sequins and varnish in the world to my husband and best friend, Patrick Murillo. I am so blessed to have you in my life. I love, love, love you! Thank you for your patience and having sharp critical thinking skills when I didn't. Much love to our kids: To DeAngelo for making me sit in the chair and write, and to Maya for letting me use her as a dress form on a moment's notice.

Muchas gracias to my parents and other family members—my sister, Theresa Cano, most of all!

Lots of hugs and high fives to the team at Duncan Enterprises, *The Arizona Republic, Good Morning Arizona,* my friends in the crafting community, and my craft group—The Phoenix Fridas. A debt of gratitude goes to the models, and the contributors who helped me make this project the best it could be.

A good karma glitter shrine goes out to my agents at WMA, Erin Malone and Scott Wachs. You are an awesome team!

Mil gracias to Janome for the use of the Memory Craft 11000, and to Laurie Notraro for writing a fabulous foreword, even though it had to be cut for space. I have it framed in my studio!

Big up to John Samora for the muy perfecto photography. Saving the best for last, my editors Rosy Ngo, Courtney Conroy, and the staff at Potter Craft. I am so proud to have written this book under your helm!

ABOUT THE AUTHOR

KATHY CANO-MURILLO, the Crafty Chica, lives in Phoenix, AZ and is an admitted craftaholic. She not only has tasted three kinds of glitter, sipped her paint water, used a glue stick for lip balm, and flaunts two nasty glue-gun burn scars, but she also took her formerly gorgeous living room and turned it into the family art studio. She has appeared on HGTV, HGTV Canada, LifetimeTV.com, and the DIY Network. She is a professional craft designer, and a national craft columnist for the *Arizona Republic*. She has written six other books, including *Crafty Chica's Art de la Soul: Glittery Ideas to Liven Up Your Life*, *The Crafty Chica Collection*, *La Casa Loca: Latino Style Comes Home*, and the popular tween Crafty Diva series. Kathy has her own line of Crafty Chica art supplies that are for sale in craft stores around the country and on her website, CraftyChica.com. The site receives more than 3 million hits a month. Her debut novel comes out in 2009.

PATRICK MURILLO is the illustrator of this book, and Kathy's husband. He has designed merchandise for HarperCollins, Lowe's Home Improvement Stores, the Crafty Chica product line, and is known for his comical Dia de Los Muertos sculptures and paintings. When he isn't in the family's living-room-turned-art-studio, he writes and records reggae en español. Patrick and Kathy have two kids, DeAngelo and Maya, and four Chihuahuas, Ozzy, Bianca, Cha-Cha, and Bootsie. Visit his website at www.patrickmurillo.com.

JOHN SAMORA is a commercial photographer based in Phoenix. His clients include Fender Musical Instruments, Capitol Records, *Sunset Magazine*, *Time*, *National Geographic*, *Glamour*, and more. He also fronts the blues band, Big Nick and the Gila Monsters. His website is www.johnsamora.com.

INDEX

TALK TO ME! If you make even one project in this book, I am super proud of you! So much that I want to see your work and post it on my website. Send pictures! I want to hear your sewing stories, too. Visit my website, CraftyChica.com to send them over. I'll also be posting new sewing projects, tips, wild art, expansions, and variations on the ideas in this book. Let's keep the party going!